Editor
Ellyn Siskind

Editorial Project Manager
Mara Ellen Guckian

Managing Editor
Ina Massler Levin, M.S. Ed.

Illustrator
Kelly McMahon

Cover Artist
Barb Lorseyedi

Art Director
CJae Forshay

Art Manager
Kevin Barnes

Imaging
Rosa C. See

Publisher
Mary D. Smith, M.S. Ed.

Math Practice for BEGIN

Pre K–K

Author

Shirley B. Spriegel, M.S. Ed.

Teacher Created Resources

Teacher Created Resources, Inc.
6421 Industry Way
Westminster, CA 92683
www.teachercreated.com
ISBN-1-4206-3115-2
©2005 Teacher Created Resources, Inc.
Made in U.S.A.

Table of Contents

Introduction

Here it is! *Math Practice for Beginners* is a simple, easy-to-use introduction to basic mathematical concepts. This workbook will promote effective learning by providing successful experiences with numbers right from the very beginning. It is important that early efforts at learning to use numbers be positive ones, as numbers will play a significant role in students' daily lives.

Our society depends on numbers to help communicate ideas. Numbers are all around us, and young children show a great curiosity about them. Early learning experiences are the building blocks for later stages of the children's number concept development in mathematics.

Extensive use of concrete objects is the foundation of teaching students about numbers and reinforces the concept that numerals are written symbols for numbers of things. Experiences with concrete materials help to provide a stimulating environment while encouraging children to experiment and discover mathematical patterns for themselves.

Those who have studied children and developmental psychology realize that young children are at the concrete stage in their development. That is, they relate to objects—tangible things that they can see and feel. Only after successfully completing this stage will they be ready to deal with the more abstract concept of the number symbol as a representation for a number of things.

In addition to working with concrete objects, young children need to develop the correct number sequence through rote oral counting. Through repetition, they hear the order and patterns in our number system.

This workbook has been designed to be developmental, sequential, and appropriate for young children.

How to Use This Book

This workbook is designed to be user-friendly. All lessons should follow the same general plan:

- Begin each lesson using concrete objects.

- Proceed to experiences on a semi-concrete level, including illustrations and drawings.

- Complete the lesson with work on the abstract level, utilizing the workbook page. The objective for each workbook page is indicated in the top right hand corner of each page. **The workbook page is always the culminating activity**.

Concrete objects should be used daily to help students learn about numbers. Simple, everyday items such as buttons, paper clips, plastic disks, or pieces of cereal can be counted and manipulated. Additional suggestions are given on page six of this book. Alternative counters are provided at the back of this book. These manipulative objects can be colored or copied onto colored paper before cutting them out. If possible, laminate them for durability.

The first ten lessons (pages 11 to 20) address following directions and will help the students get "tuned in" to listening to the teacher. Lessons on pages 11–30 do not include student directions. The teacher directions are given below a dashed line on each page. Fold the directions under before copying these pages for students. These are oral exercises. Read these directions to students, one line at a time. Allow ample time to carry out the instruction before proceeding to the next line. These lessons also teach students relational vocabulary words used to indicate direction, size, and left and right.

The next ten lessons (pages 21 to 30) are designed to introduce the students to the concept of one-to-one correspondence. *One-to-one correspondence* is the basis for counting and is essential for mastering computational skills. It involves understanding that one object in a set is the same number as one object in a different set, whether or not characteristics are similar. Children can match pencils to books, chairs to children, buttons to cards, straws to milk cartons, or whatever is available. To help introduce one-to-one correspondence, the teacher could distribute five craft sticks and five buttons to each child. The teacher could say, "Put three buttons in a row on your desk. Put one button on each craft stick. Now put five buttons in a row on your desk. Put a button on each craft stick." Then continue with other directions using the sticks and buttons.

How to Use This Book (cont.)

After the students have had experiences leading to the understanding of one-to-one correspondence, the numbers 1 to 10 are introduced along with experiences in counting objects and writing the numbers. As concrete objects are used, it is important that there be a direct correlation between the manipulative activities and the worksheet used as the culminating activity. (Teacher note: The term "numeral" means the written symbol indicating a "number" of things. In this book, however, we will use the term "number" to indicate both the numeral and the number of objects.)

Preparation for addition, addition sentences, subtraction, and subtraction sentences will be more fun and more easily understood when concrete materials, games, and singing songs with numbers are a natural part of the curriculum. Children will memorize basic addition and subtraction facts because they understand the processes, have the facts organized according to logical structure, and have meaningful practice with objects.

Math Practice for Beginners also encourages students to develop mental images of the mathematical processes. Incidental problem solving helps children to "think numbers." For example, as an introduction to addition, the teacher might say, "There are four books here and six children. How many more books will we need?" Or, "We need one spoon for each child. How many spoons will we need?" Or, "There are five chairs and seven children. How many more chairs will we need?" Another problem could be, "There are three boys here and four boys over there. How many is that altogether?" To have fun with subtraction, tell the children to line up six chocolate chips and eat two. Then ask, "How many are left?" What fun! (Allergy Alert: Check for student allergies before using food in counting activities.)

When introducing vertical addition and subtraction, the teacher can write the numbers on the chalkboard or dry erase board while the students use counters at their desks or tables to illustrate the problem.

As an additional enhancement to your math lessons, you may wish to incorporate the vocabulary cards included on pages seven through ten. You may want to prominently display the word/s associated with a particular lesson during the lesson itself, use them to reinforce oral directions, or incorporate them into Language Arts lessons.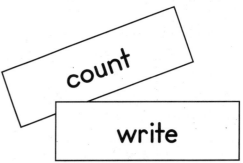

The teacher's good judgment and knowledge of her/his children will result in many more meaningful word problems than could be included in any manual.

This book contains 190 lessons, more than enough for an entire school year and a successful beginning in mathematics for all of your students.

Suggested Materials List

Concrete Objects

- beans
- blocks
- buttons
- cereal pieces
- chocolate chips
- craft sticks
- crayons
- drinking straws

- macaroni
- nails
- paper clips
- paper cups
- paper fasteners
- pencils
- pennies
- plastic cars

- plastic utensils
- poker chips
- raisins
- screws
- seeds
- shells
- stones or gravel
- toothpicks

Semi-concrete Objects

- chalkboard drawings
- dots on cards

- feltboard cutouts
- illustrations of objects

- lines on papers
- pictures

Note: Beginning on page 141, extensive use is made of O-shaped cereal. It is represented by this symbol ⊙ . It has been found that children's interest levels will be higher and more prolonged if they are able to eat the counters at the end of the lesson! It is always important to check lists of food allergies before using foods as counters.

Beginning on page 202 of this book are pages of manipulative objects and number cards which can be cut out and laminated. The manipulatives can be used in a variety of activities including counting practice and in games. The number cards can also be used for counting and writing practice as well as for making number sentences. It is suggested that these materials be kept in sandwich bags for easy storage and access. Use the award certificate on page 201 when students have completed the lessons.

Laminate and cut out these cards for use during activities.

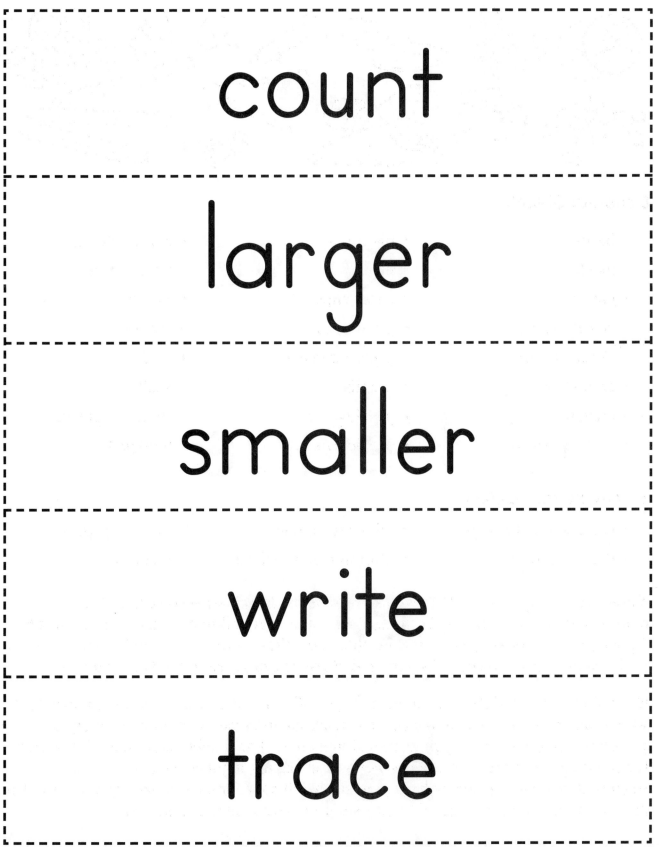

count

larger

smaller

write

trace

Laminate and cut out these cards for use during activities.

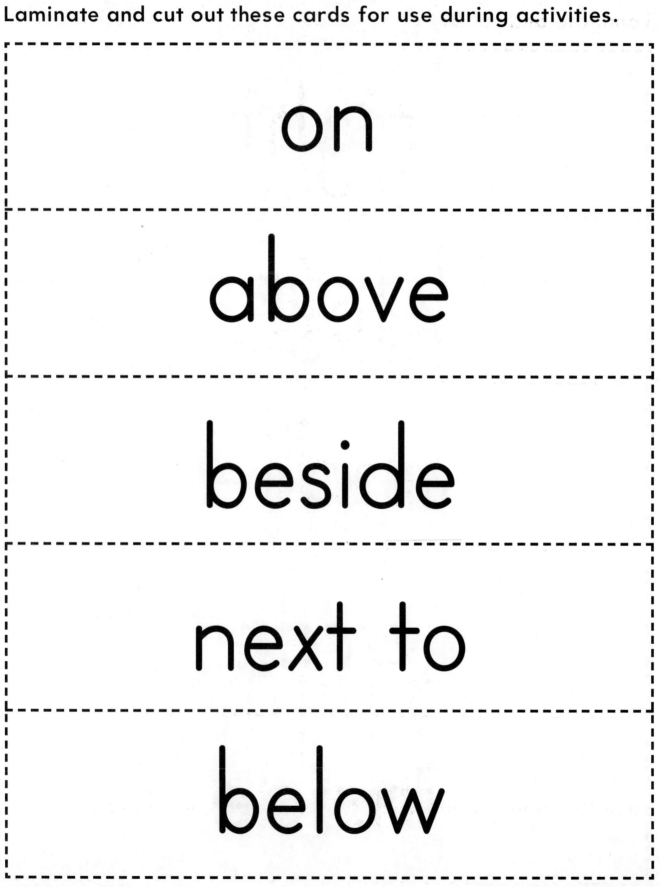

on

above

beside

next to

below

8

Laminate and cut out these cards for use during activities.

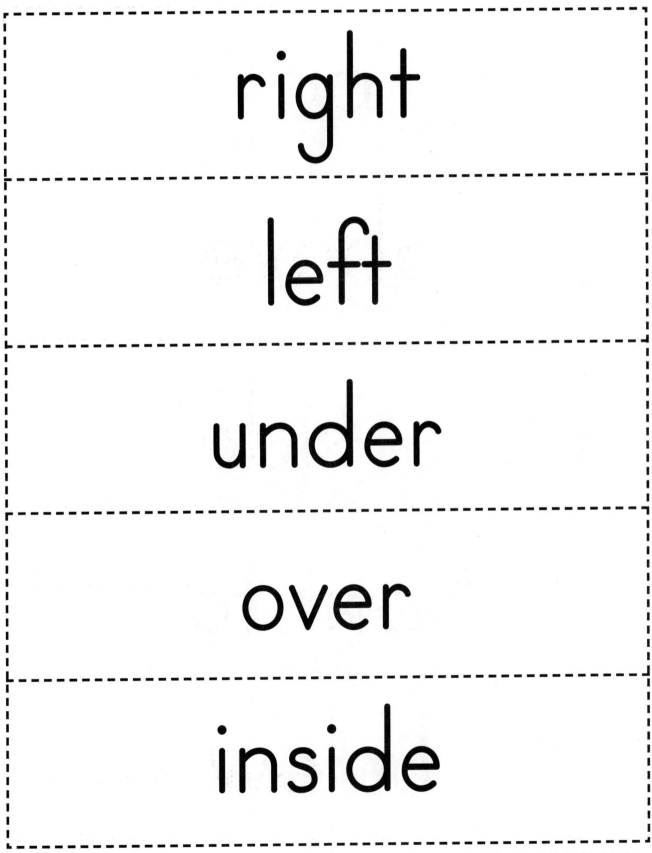

right

left

under

over

inside

Laminate and cut out these cards for use during activities.

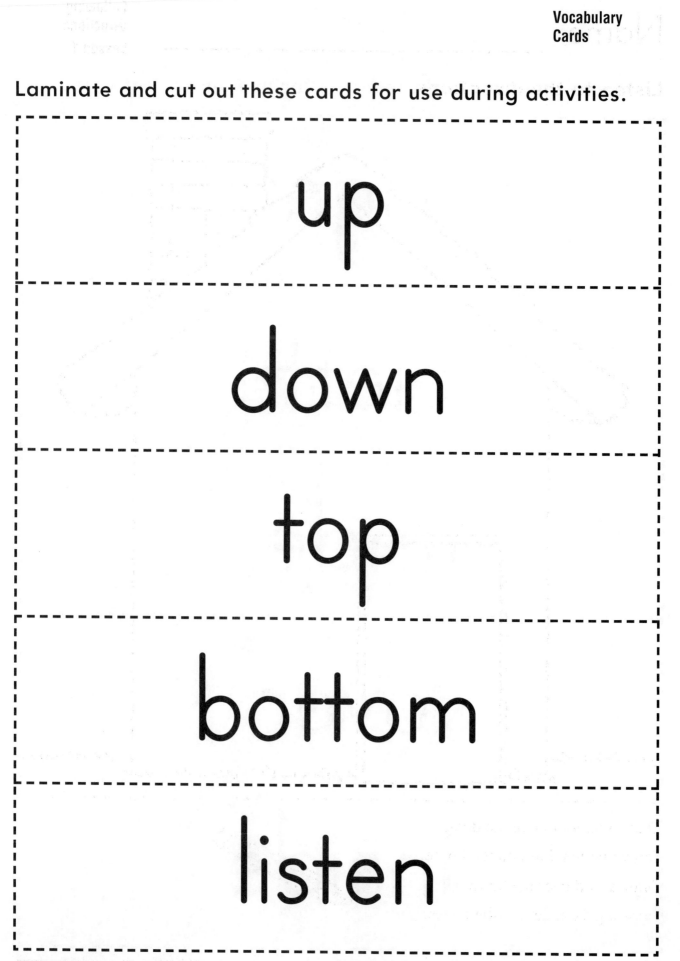

up

down

top

bottom

listen

10

Name _____

Listen to the directions.

Draw a doorknob on the door.

Draw two windows on the house.

Draw a bird over the house.

Draw a person next to the house.

Name _____

Listen to the directions.

- -

Draw a ball under the table.

Draw a box on the table.

Draw a cloud over the table.

Draw a line below the table.

Draw a triangle beside the table.

Name _____

Listen to the directions.

- -

Draw a flower beside the doghouse.

Draw a bone below the doghouse.

Draw a sun above the doghouse.

Draw a line next to the doghouse.

Draw a bird above the doghouse.

Name _____

Listen to the directions.

- -

Draw an X under the person who is *up*.

Draw a line over the person who is *down*.

Draw a sun at the top of the page.

Put some grass at the bottom of the page.

Name _____

Listen to the directions.

- -

Draw a line from the larger dog to the smaller dog.

Draw a line from the larger triangle to the smaller triangle.

Draw a line from the smaller ball to the larger ball.

Name _____

Listen to the directions.

- -

Draw a circle at the top of the ladder.

Draw an X at the middle of the ladder.

Draw a box at the bottom of the ladder.

Draw a person next to the ladder.

Name _____

Listen to the directions.

- -

Draw a flag at the top of the sailboat.

Draw a circle at the middle of the sail.

Draw a fish below the sailboat.

Name _____

Listen to the directions.

- -

Draw a circle in one hand.

Draw a square in the other hand.

Put a face on the person.

Put ears on the sides of the head.

Name _____

Listen to the directions.

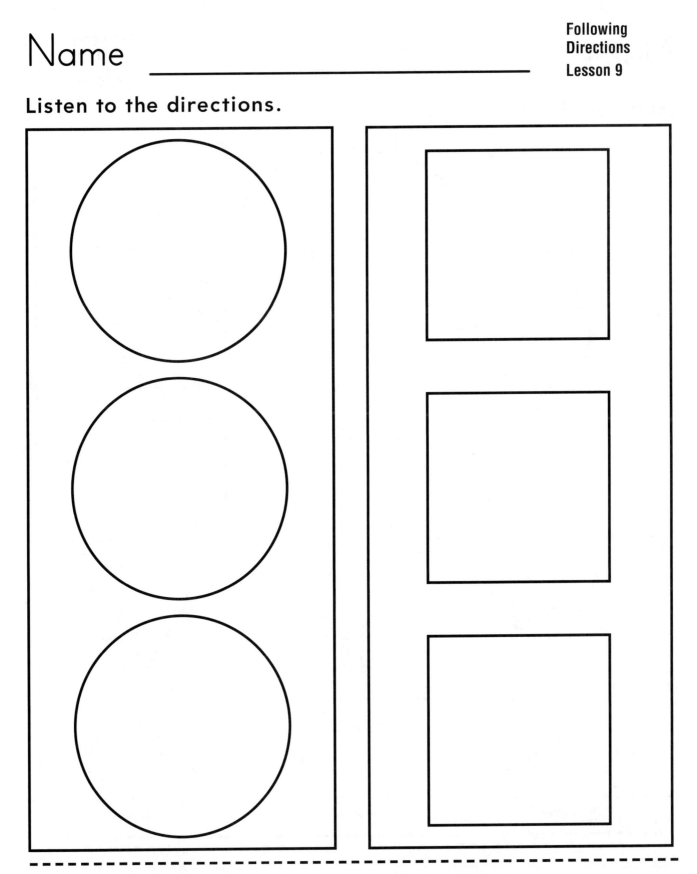

Color the top circle red.

Color the middle circle yellow.

Color the bottom circle green.

Color the middle square purple.

Color the bottom square orange.

Color the top square blue.

Name _____

Listen to the directions.

Color the top circle blue.

Color the bottom circle purple.

Color the middle square green.

Color the top square yellow.

Color the bottom square red.

Color the tree on the left green.

Color the tree on the right brown.

Color the apple on the left yellow.

Color the apple on the right red.

Name _____

Listen to the directions.

Draw a flag for each pole.

Draw a box for each table.

Draw a ball for each chair.

Name _____

Listen to the directions.

- -

Draw an apple for each dish.

Draw a flag for each person.

Draw a carrot above each rabbit.

Listen to the directions.

Draw a flower for each stem.

Draw a roof for each house.

Draw a circle for each triangle.

Draw a box for each wagon.

Name _____

Listen to the directions.

Draw a crayon for each rectangle.

Draw a string for each balloon.

Draw a stamp for each envelope.

Draw flames for each pile of wood.

Name _____

Listen to the directions.

Draw a face for each kite.

Draw a balloon for each person.

Draw a sail for each boat.

Name _____

Listen to the directions.

- -

Draw a flower for each pot.

Draw a smile for each face.

Draw a shoe for each foot.

Draw a head for each chick.

Name _____

Listen to the directions.

- -

Draw a handle for each cup.

Draw a boat for each sail.

Draw a balloon for each clown.

Draw a circle in each square.

Name _____

Listen to the directions.

- -

Draw a yolk for each egg.

Draw a chimney and a window for each house.

Draw a circle around each star.

Draw an egg for each duck.

Name _____

Listen to the directions.

- -

Draw a tail for each cat.

Draw an arrow for each heart.

Draw a candle for each cake.

Draw a bird in each birdhouse.

Name _____

Listen to the directions.

- -

Draw ice cream for each cone.

Draw ears for each rabbit.

Draw a trunk for each tree.

Draw a tail for each mouse.

Name _____

Circle the number of objects in each box. Count one car.

Name _____

Trace, write, and say the number one.

Write the number of objects in each box on the line.

_____	_____
_____	_____

Name _____

Trace, write, and say the number one.

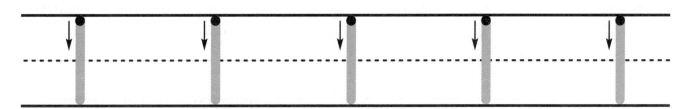

Write the number of objects in each box on the line.

Name _____

Trace, write, and say the number one.

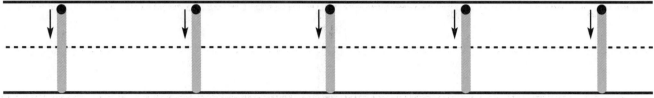

Write the number of objects in each box on the line.

Name _____

Trace, write, and say the number one.

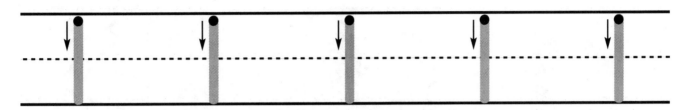

Write the number of objects in each box on the line.

Name _____

Count the clowns.

Circle the number of objects in each box.

Name _____

Practice writing the number two.

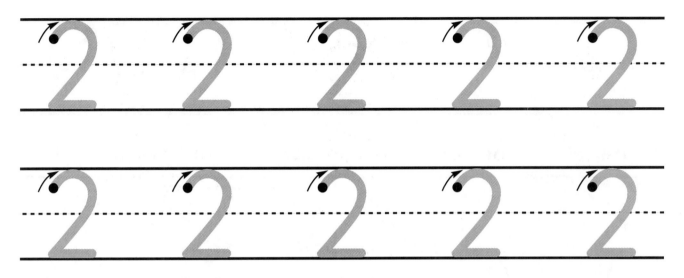

Write the number of objects in each box on the line.

Name _____

Practice writing the number two.

Write the number of objects in each box on the line.

38

Name _____

Practice writing the number two.

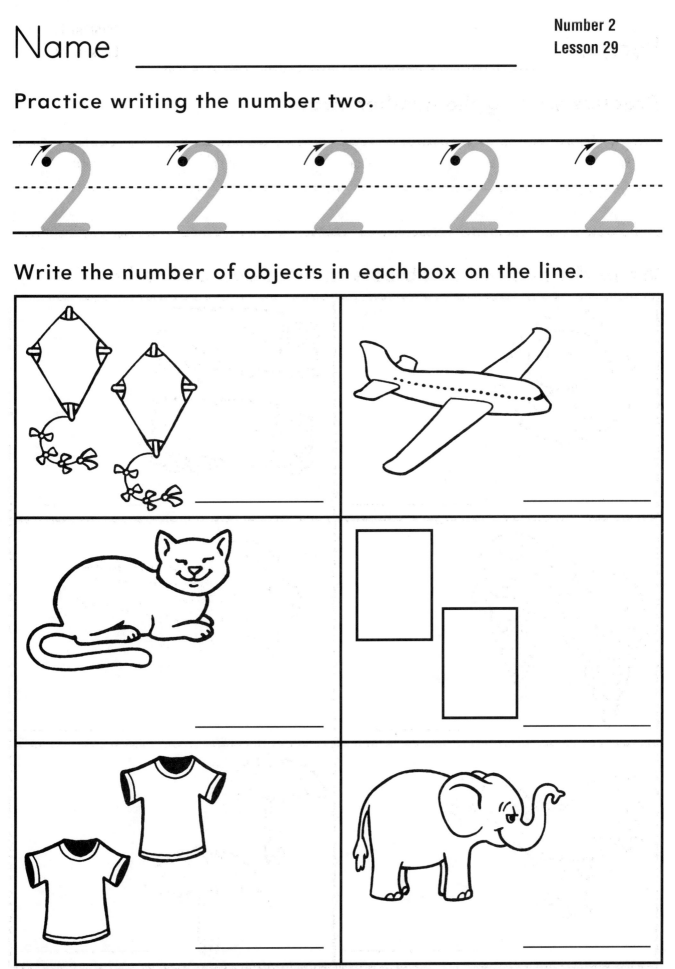

Write the number of objects in each box on the line.

Name _____

Practice writing the number two.

Write the number of objects in each box on the line.

40

Name _____

Count three ducks.

Circle the number of objects in each box.

Name _____

Trace the number three.

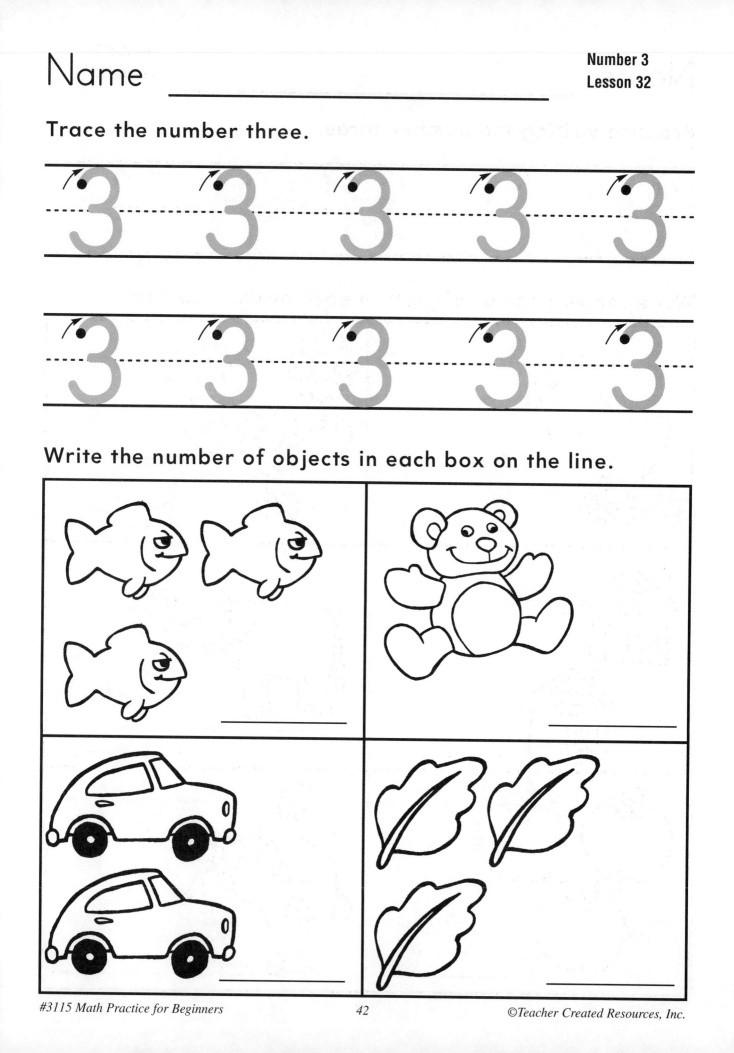

Write the number of objects in each box on the line.

Name _____

Practice writing the number three.

Write the number of objects in each box on the line.

Name _____

Trace the number three.

3 3 3 3 3

Write the number of objects in each box on the line.

44

Name _____

Trace and cut out the numbers at the bottom.
Count the animals and paste the correct number in the box.

Name _____

Trace the numbers.

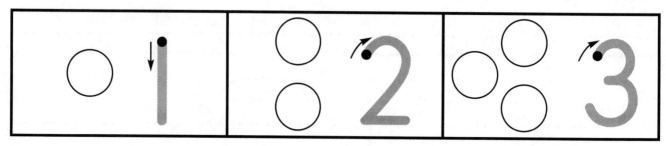

Write the number of objects in each box on the line.

Name _____

Trace the number three.

Write the number of objects in each box on the line.

Name _____

Writing 1, 2, 3
Lesson 38

Trace and write the numbers on the lines.

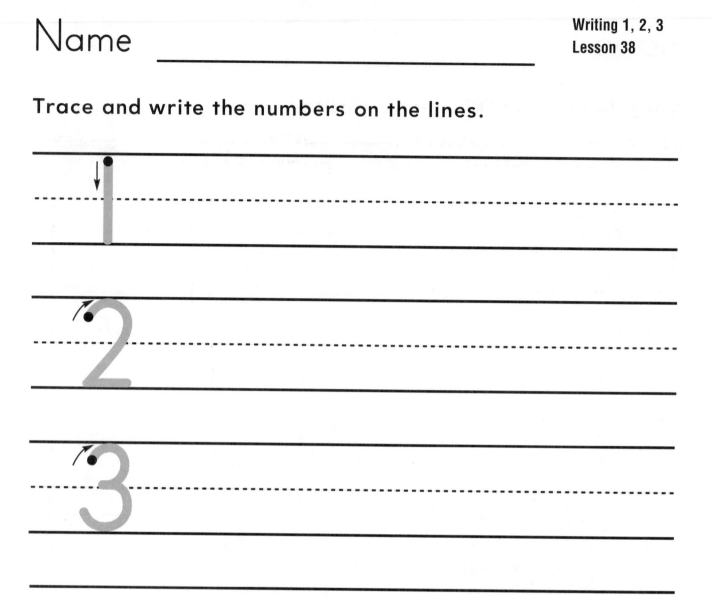

Count the animals and write the number on the line.

Name _____

Trace and cut out the numbers at the bottom.
Count the faces and paste the correct number in the box.

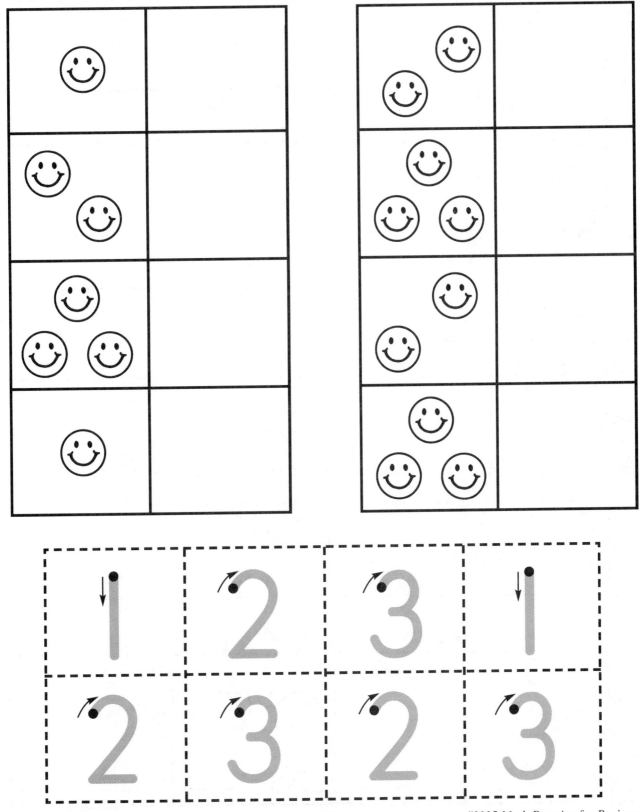

Name _____

Write the number of objects in each box on the line.

50

Name _____

Count the four frogs.

Circle the number of objects in each box.

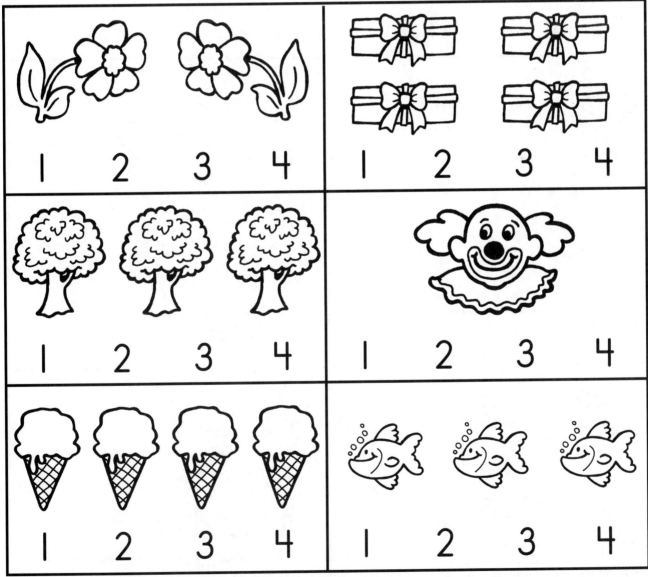

Name _____

Trace the number four.

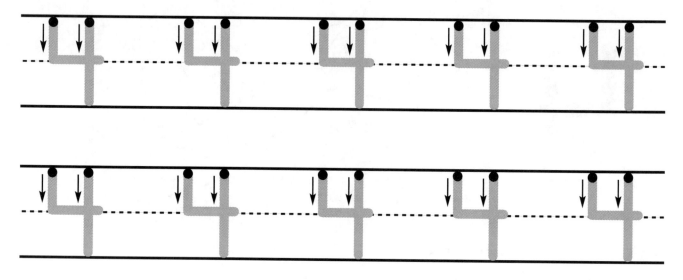

Write the number of objects in each box on the line.

Name _____

Practice writing the number four.

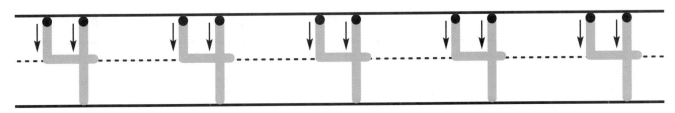

Write the number of objects in each box on the line.

Name _____

Trace and cut out the numbers at the bottom of the page.
Count the balls and paste the correct number in the box.

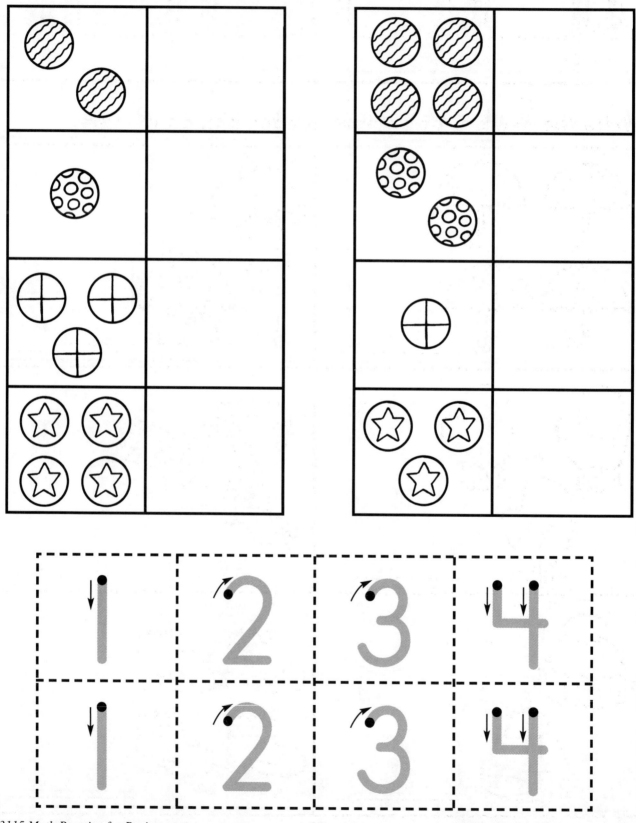

Name _____

Trace the numbers.

Write the number of objects in each box on the line.

Name _____

Trace the numbers. Write the number of sheep on the line.

Write the number of objects in each box on the line.

Name _____

Trace the numbers.

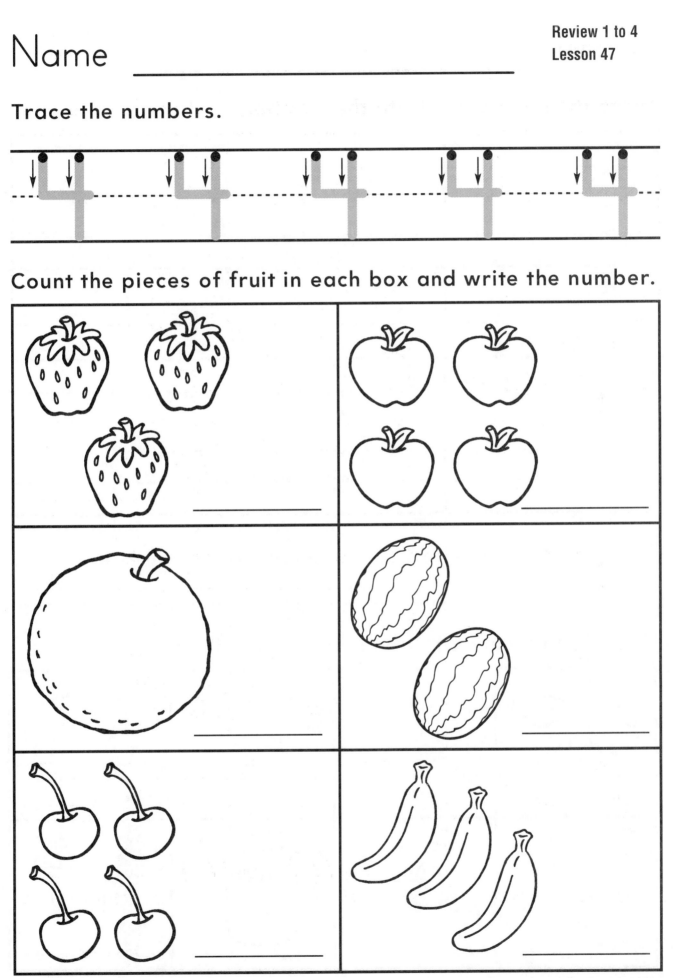

Count the pieces of fruit in each box and write the number.

Name _____

Practice writing the numbers.

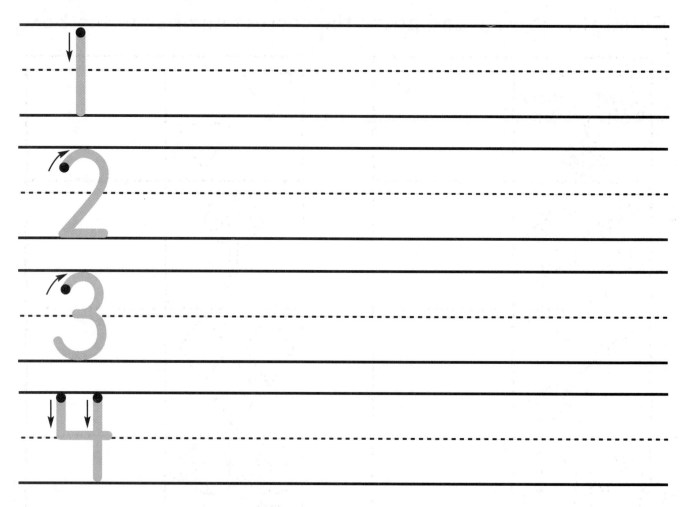

Write the number of objects in each box.

Name _____

Trace and cut out the numbers at the bottom.

Count the objects and paste the correct number in the box.

Name _____

Count the objects and write the correct number on the line.

Name _____

Count five ducks.

Circle the number of eggs in each box.

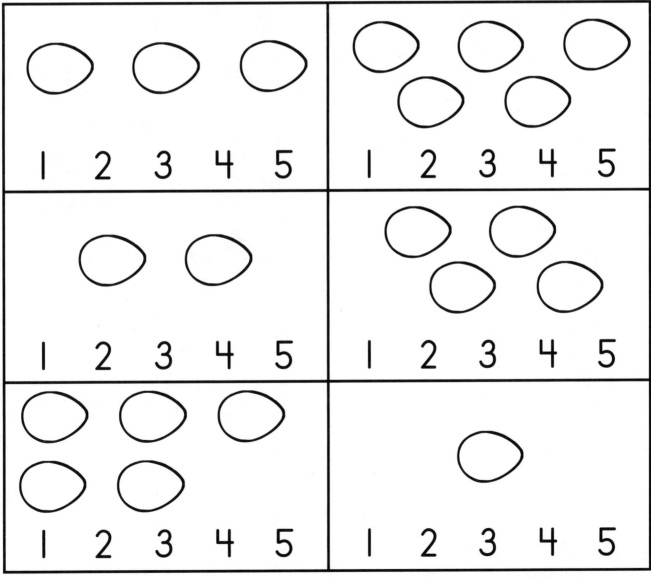

Name _____

Practice writing the number five.

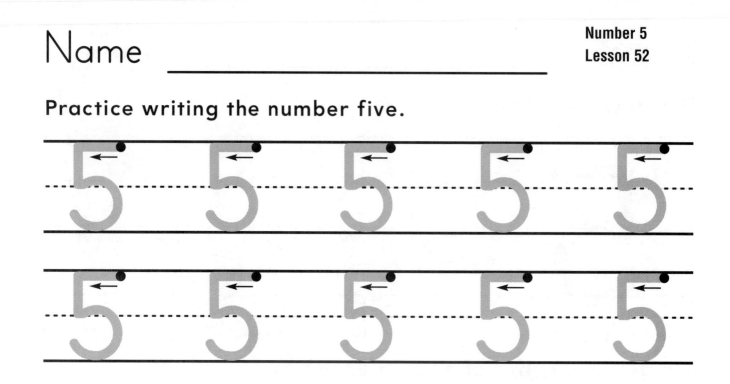

Count the animals and write the number on the line.

62

Name _____

Trace the number five.

5 5 5 5 5

Count the animals in each box and write the number.

Name _____

Trace and cut out the numbers at the bottom.

Count the shapes and paste the correct number in the box.

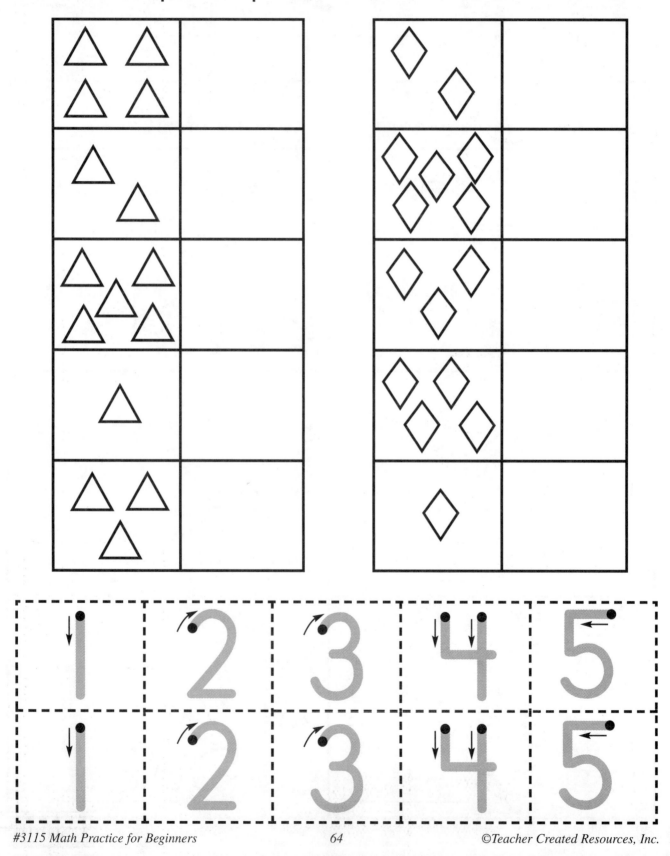

Name _____

Trace the numbers.

5   5   5   5   5

Count the instruments and write the number on the line.

Name _____

Trace the numbers.

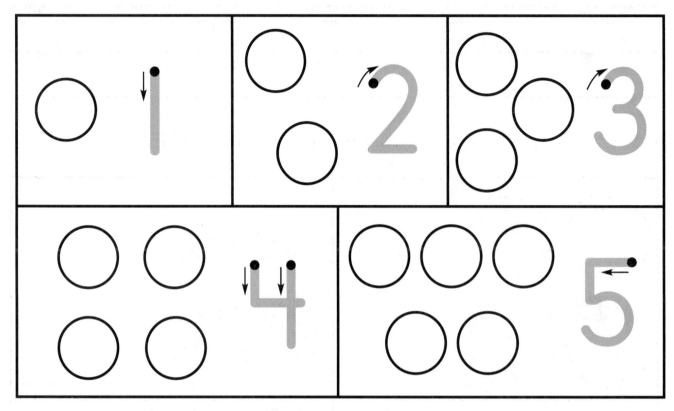

Count the items and write the number on the line.

Trace the numbers.

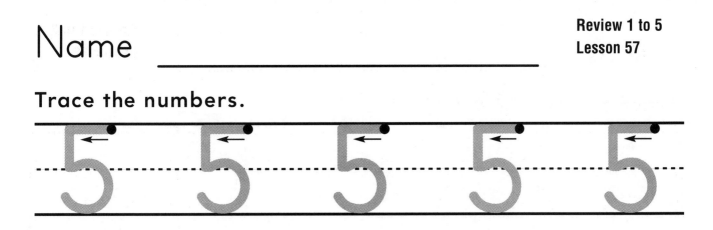

Count the fruits and write the number on the line.

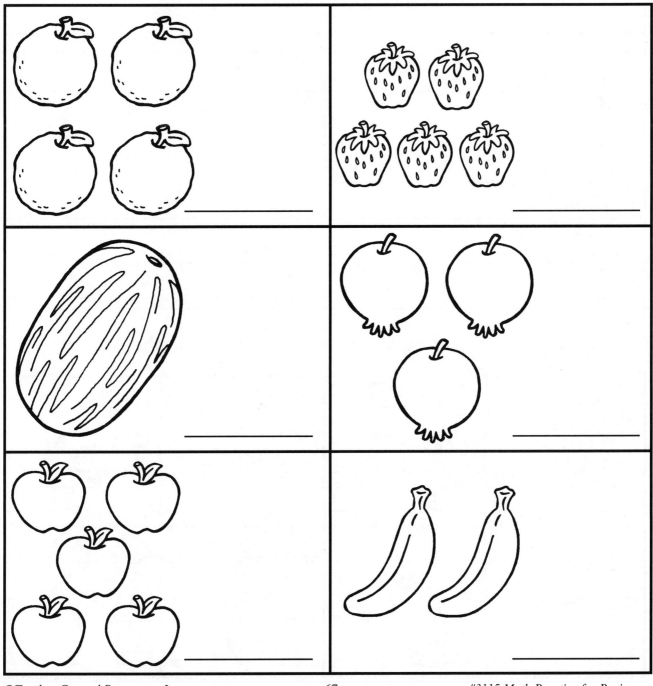

Name _____

Trace and write the numbers.

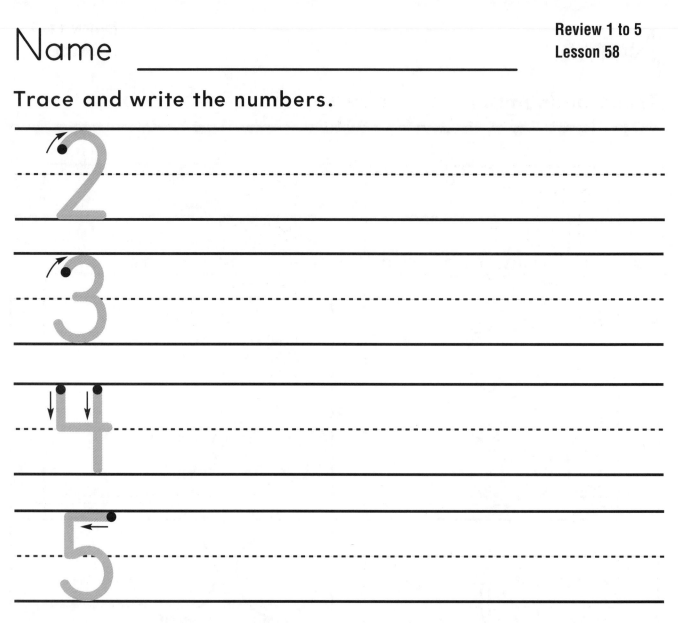

Count the desserts and write the number on the line.

Name _____

Trace and cut out the numbers at the bottom. Count the objects and paste the correct number in the box.

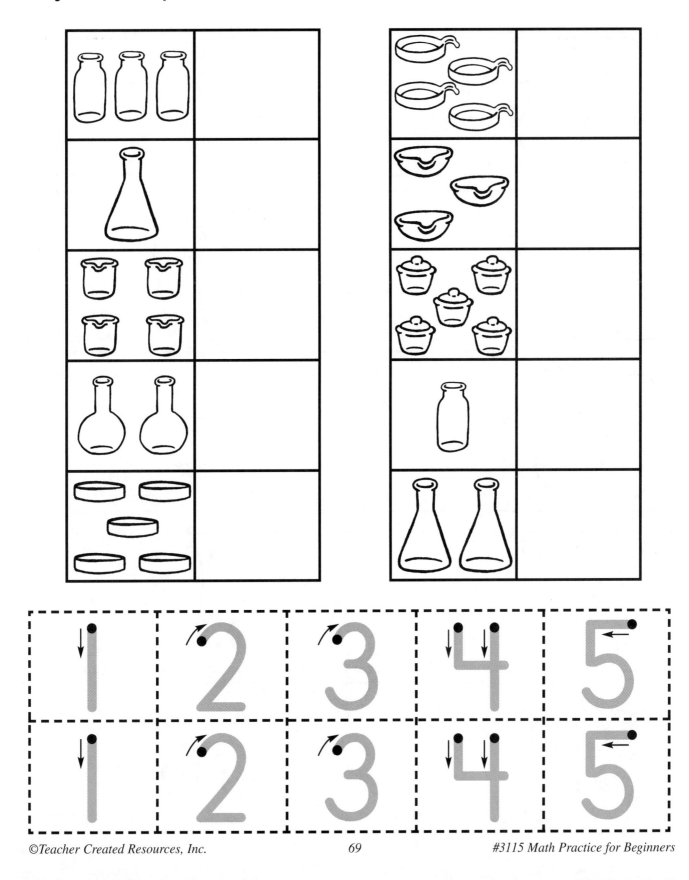

Name _____

Count the fruits and vegetables in each box. Write the number on the line.

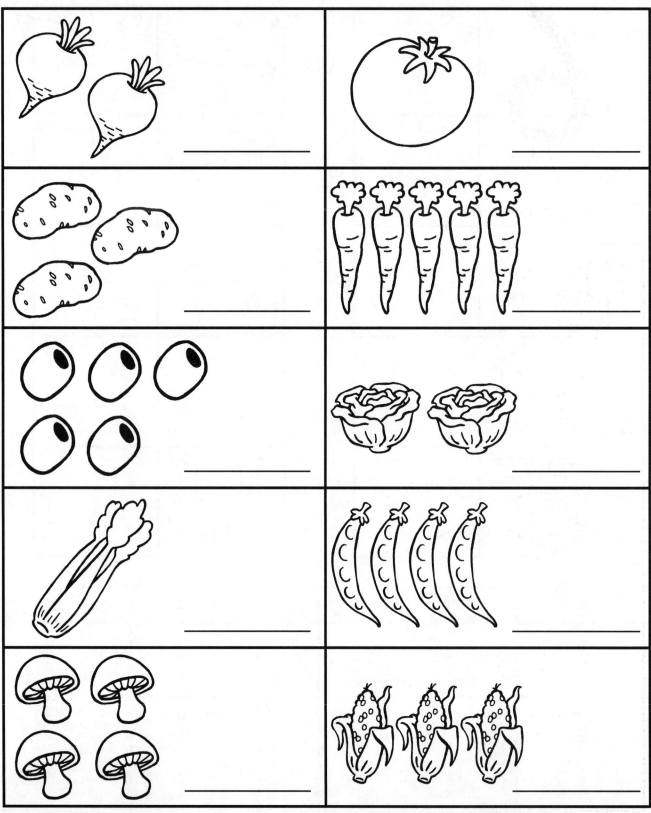

Name _____

Count six dogs.

Circle the number of bones in each box.

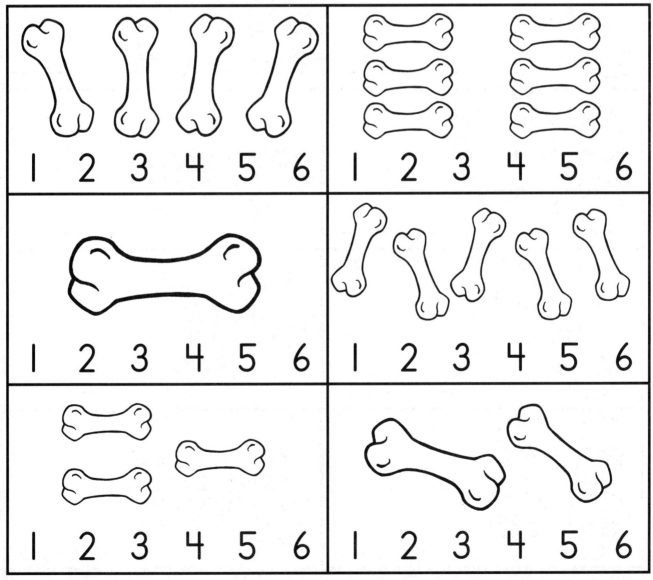

Name _____

Practice writing the number six.

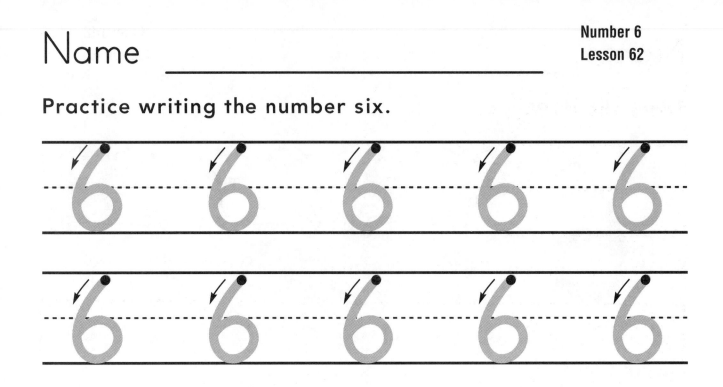

Count the flowers and write the number on the line.

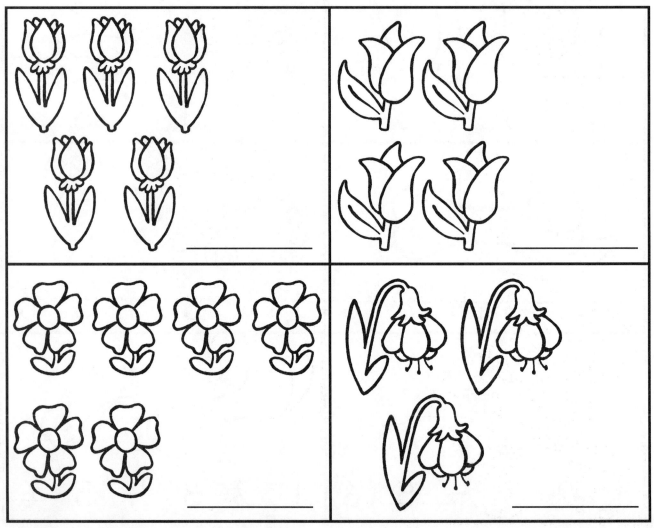

72

Name _____

Trace the numbers.

6 6 6 6 6

Write the number of balls in each box on the line.

_____   _____

_____   _____

_____   _____

Name _____

Trace and cut out the numbers at the bottom.
Count the objects and paste the correct number in the box.

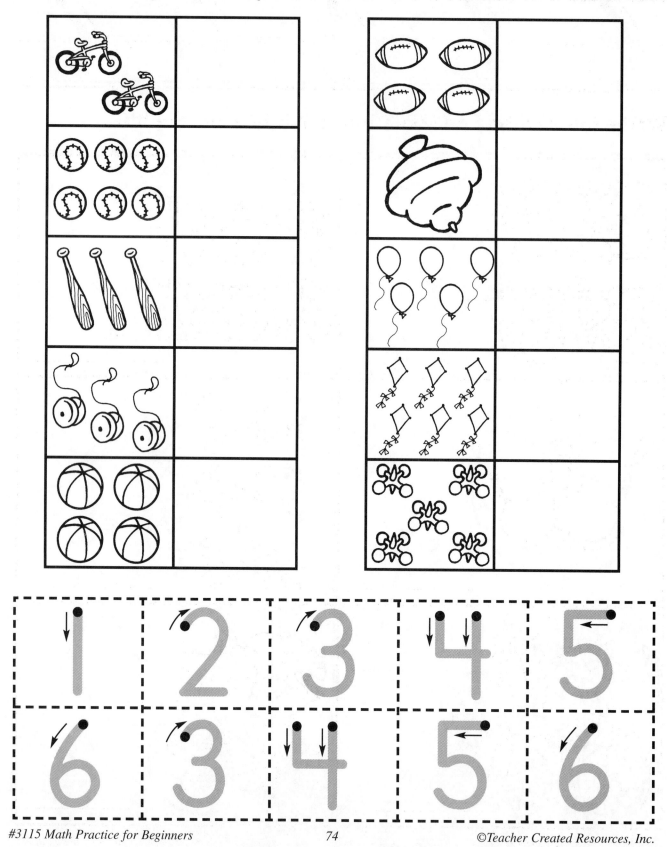

Name _____

Trace the numbers.

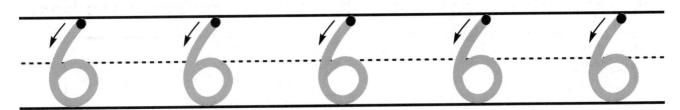

Write the number of insects in each box on the line.

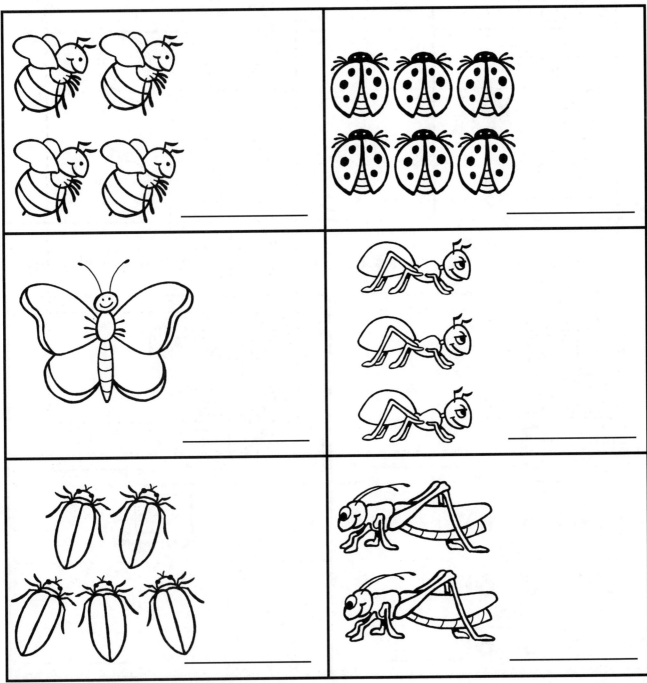

Trace the numbers.

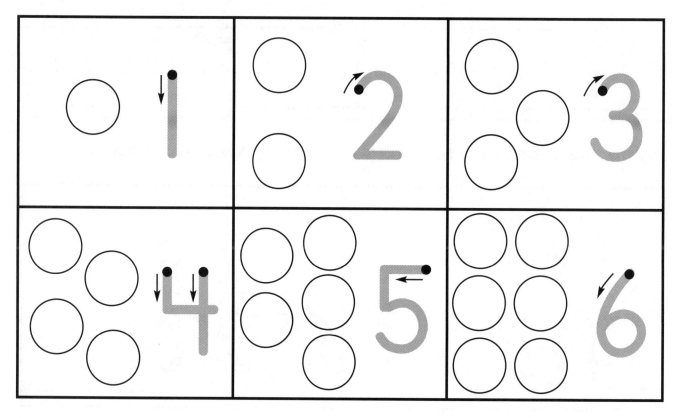

Count the cars and trucks and write the number on the line.

Name _____

Trace the numbers.

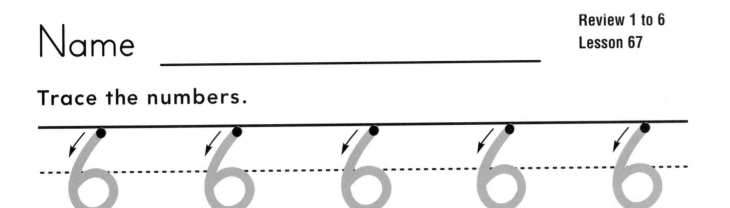

Count the animals and write the number on the line.

Name _____

Trace and write the numbers.

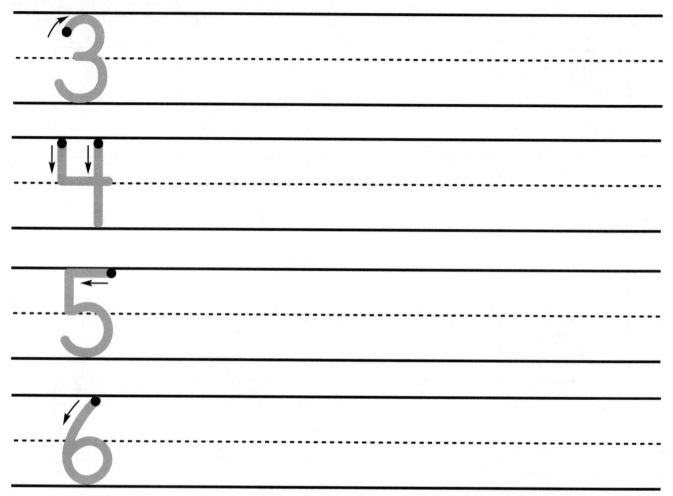

Count the shapes and write the number on the line.

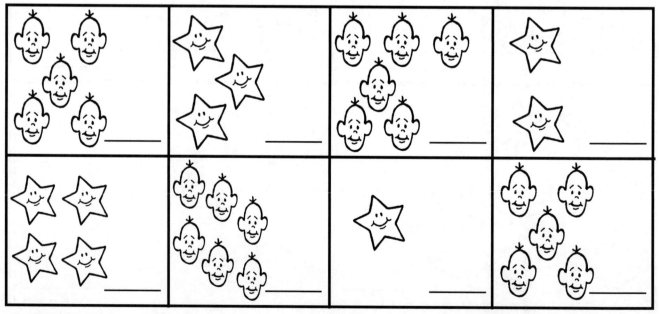

Name _____

Trace and cut out the numbers at the bottom.

Count the butterflies and paste the correct number in the box.

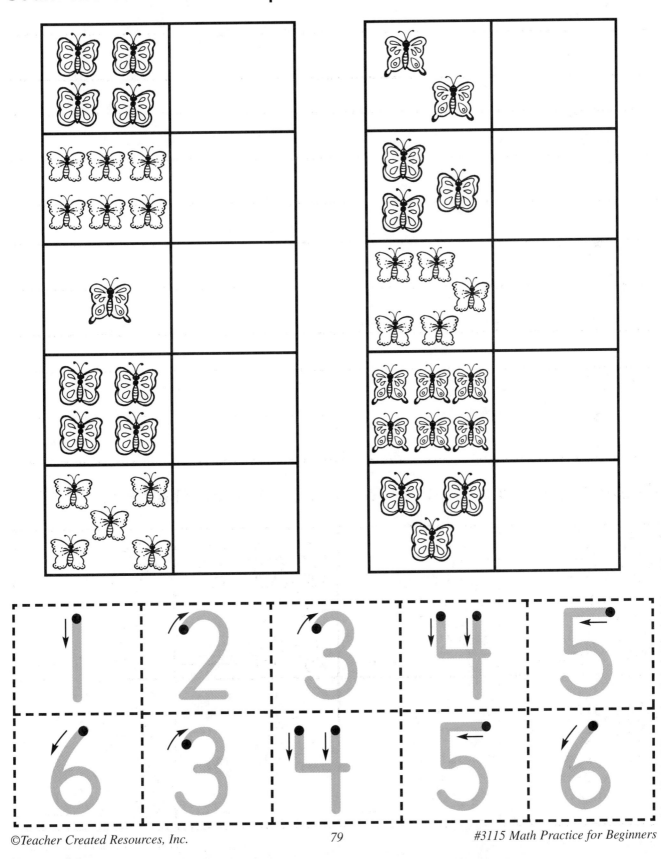

Name _____

Count the animals and write the number on the line.

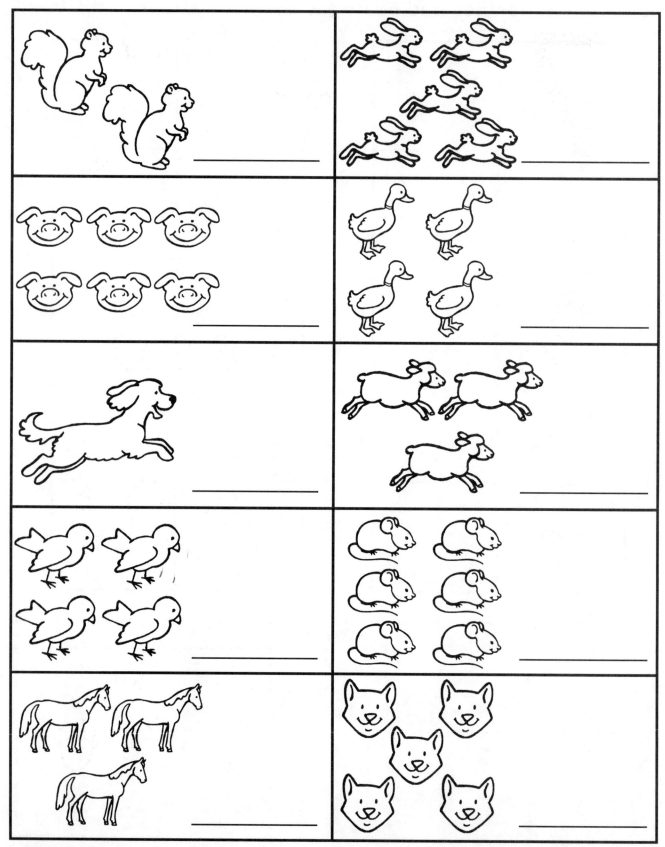

80

Name _____

Count seven squirrels.

Circle the number of acorns in each box.

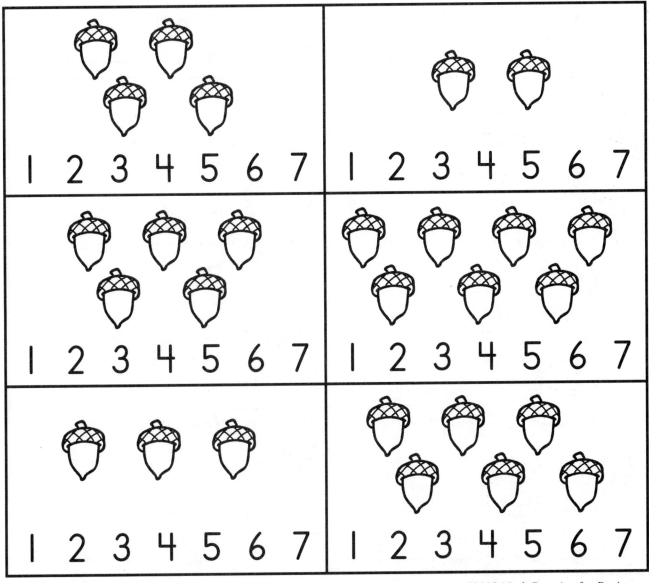

Name

Practice writing the number seven.

7   7   7   7   7

7   7   7   7   7

Write the number of objects in each box on the line.

82

Name

Trace the numbers.

7 7 7 7 7

Write the number of objects in each box on the line.

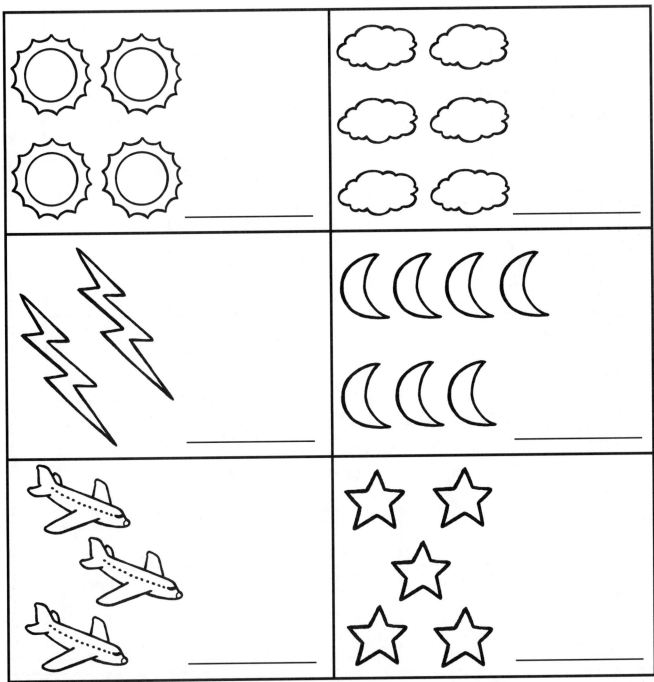

Name _____

Trace and cut out the numbers at the bottom.

Count the flowers and paste the correct number in the box.

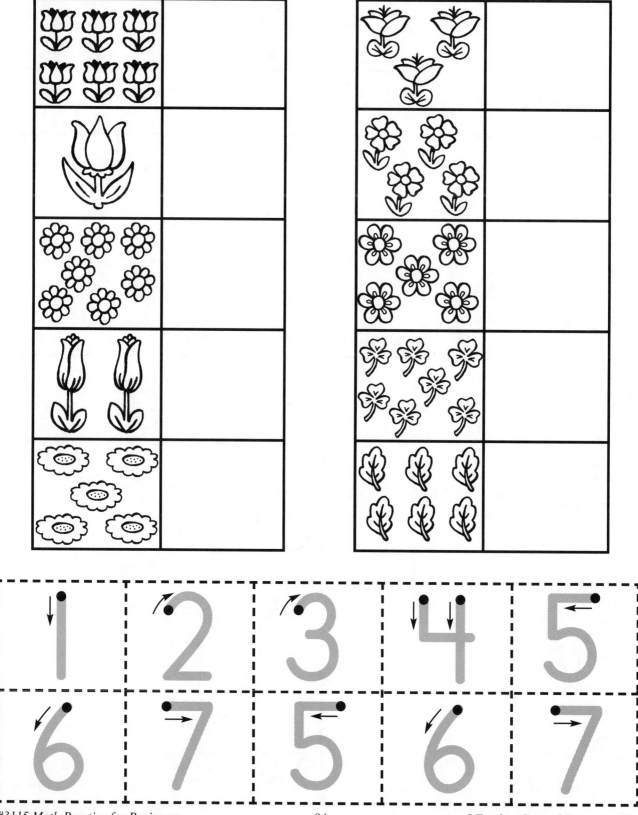

Name _____

Trace the numbers.

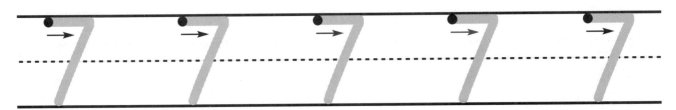

Write the number of objects in each box on the line.

Name _____

Trace the numbers in each box.

Count the balloons and write the number on the line.

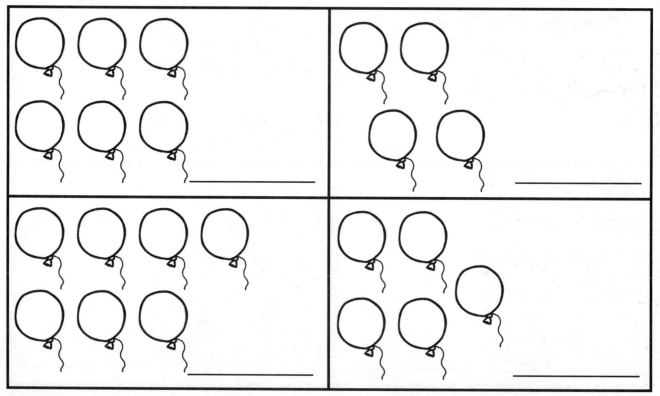

86

Name _____

Trace the numbers.

7 7 7 7 7

Count the animals and write the number on the line.

_____

_____

_____

_____

_____

_____

Name _____

Trace and write the numbers.

Count the apples and write the number on the line.

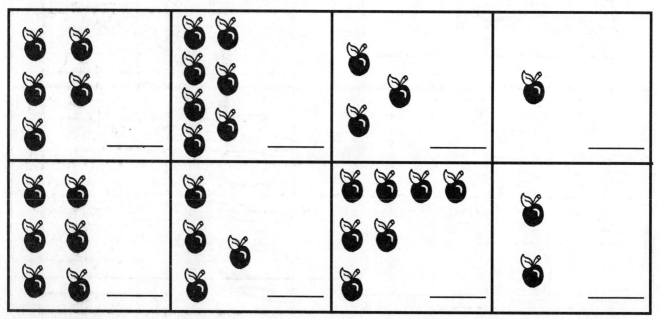

Name _____

Trace and cut out the numbers at the bottom.
Count the boats and paste the correct number in the box.

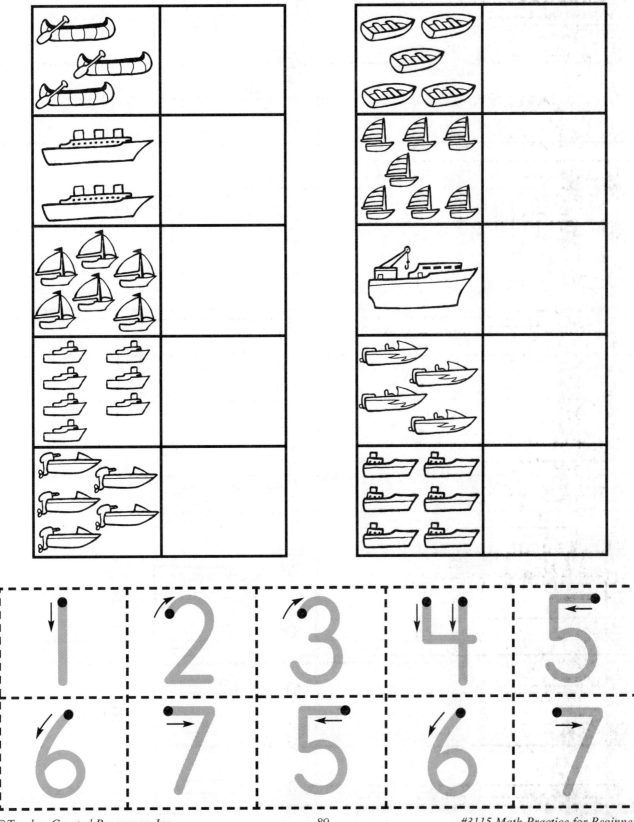

Name _____

Count the school items and write the number on the line.

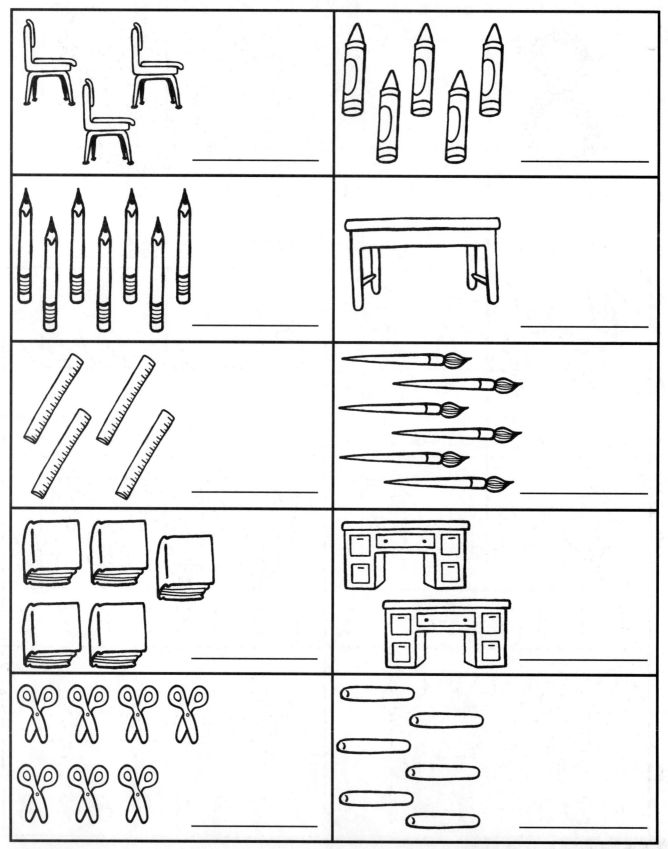

Name _____

Count eight trees.

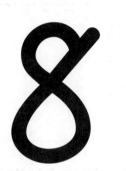

Circle the number of leaves in each box.

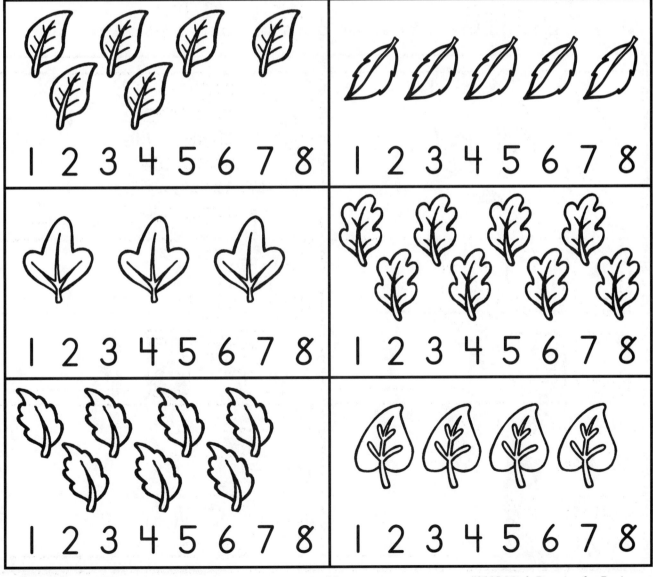

Name _____

Practice writing the number eight.

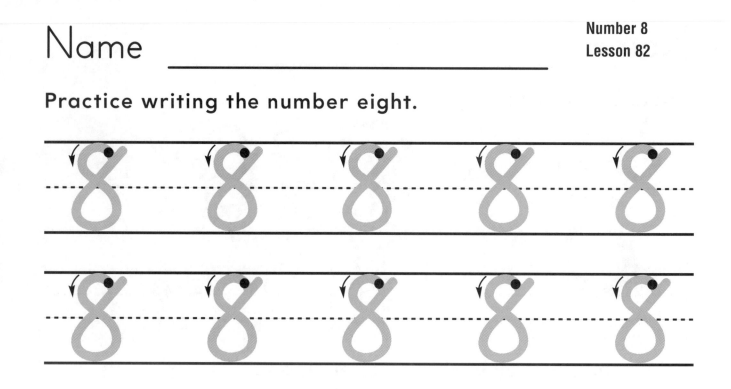

Write the number of boys or girls in each box on the line.

Name _____

Trace the number eight.

Write the number of objects in each box on the line.

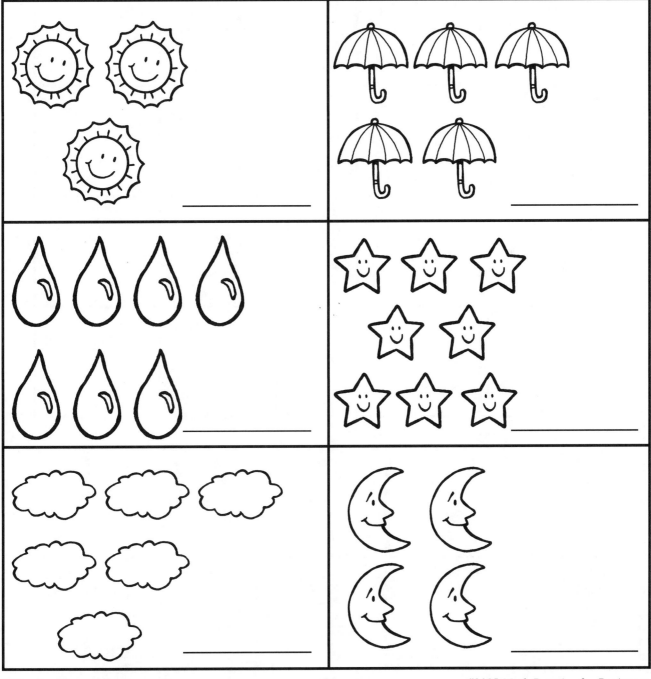

Name _____

Trace and cut out the numbers at the bottom of the page.
Count the birds and paste the correct number in the box.

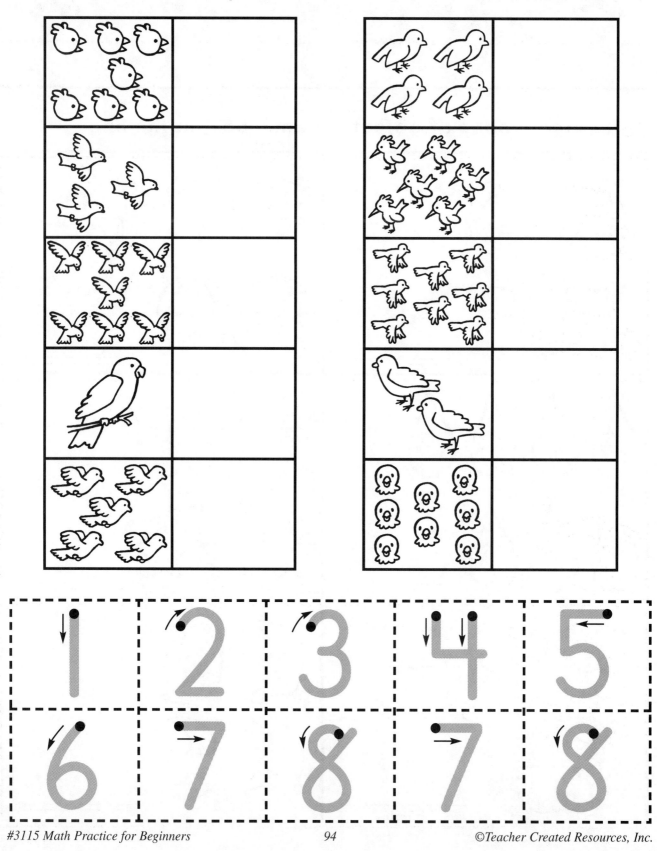

94

©Teacher Created Resources, Inc.

Name _____

Trace the numbers.

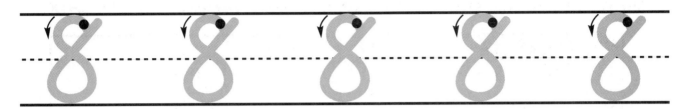

Count the objects and write the number on the line.

Name _____

Trace the numbers.

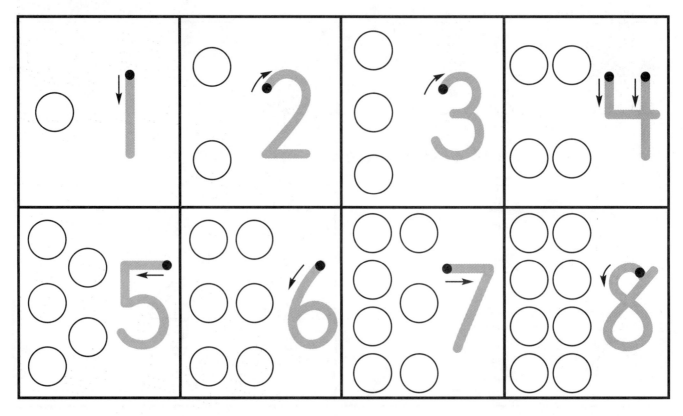

Count the animals and write the number on the line.

Name _____

Trace the numbers.

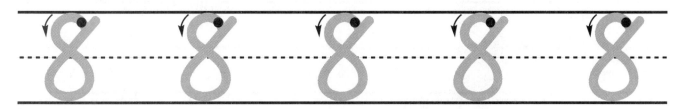

Count the vehicles and write the number on the line.

Name _____

Trace and write the numbers.

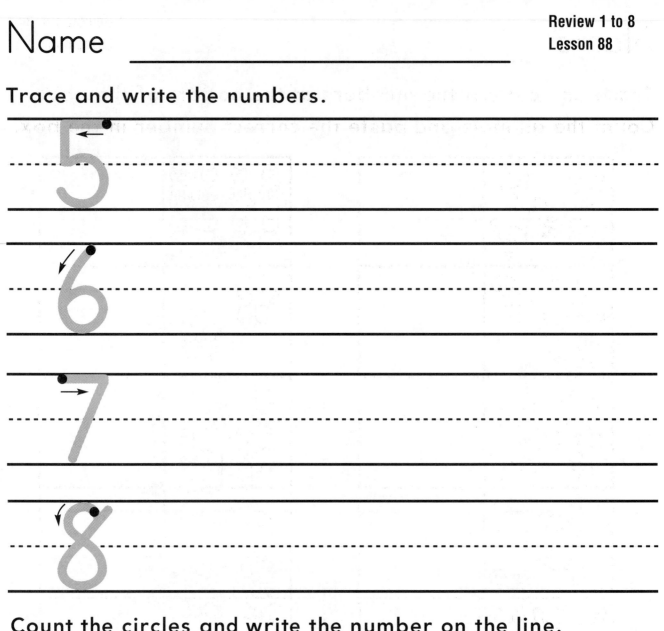

Count the circles and write the number on the line.

Name _____

Trace and cut out the numbers at the bottom of the page.
Count the animals and paste the correct number in the box.

Name _____

Count the shapes. Write the number on the line.

Count nine mice.

Circle the number of pieces of cheese in each box.

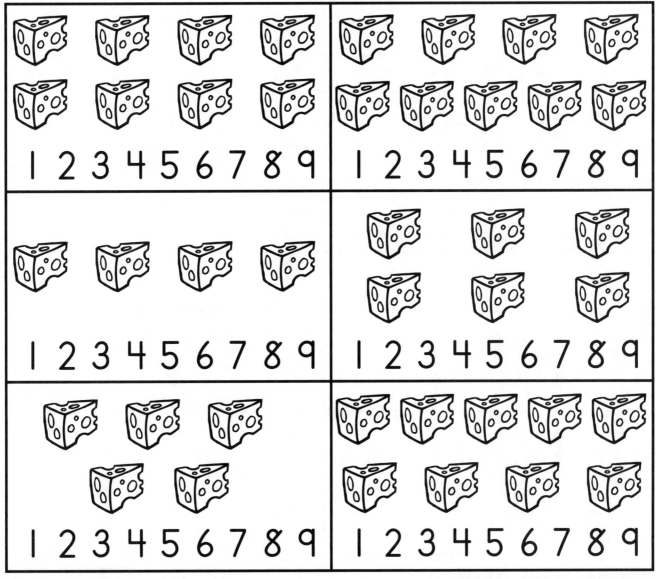

Name _____

Practice writing the number nine.

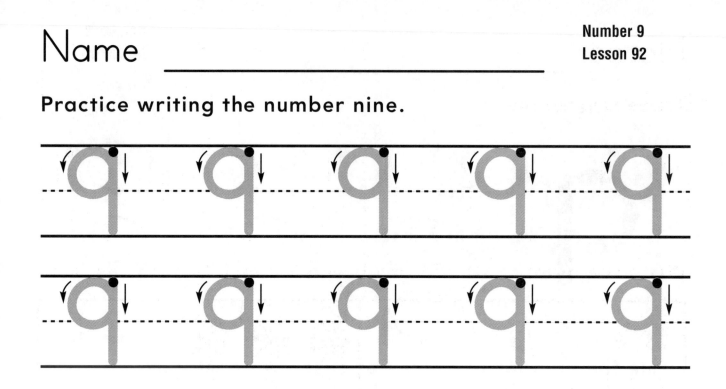

Write the number of keys and keyholes on the line.

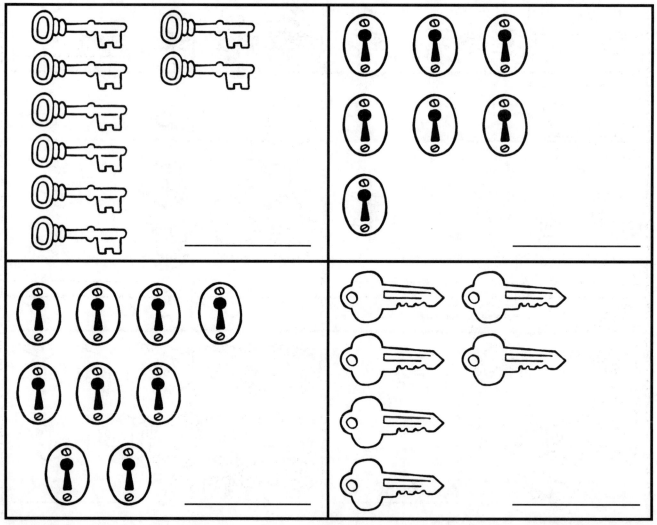

102

Name _____

Trace the numbers.

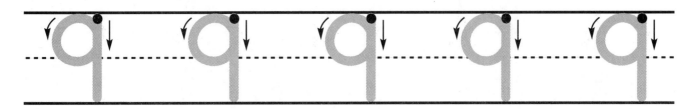

Write the number of winter objects in each box on the line.

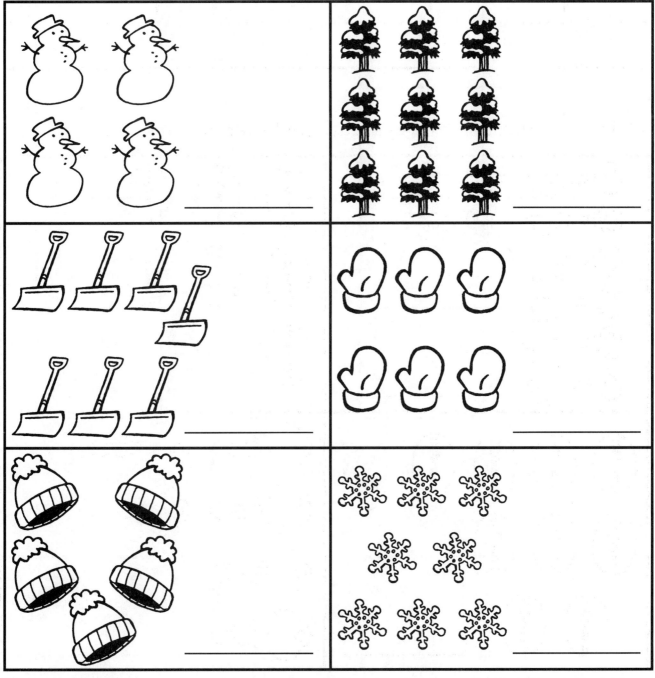

Name _____

Trace and cut out the numbers at the bottom of the page.
Count the objects and paste the correct number in the box.

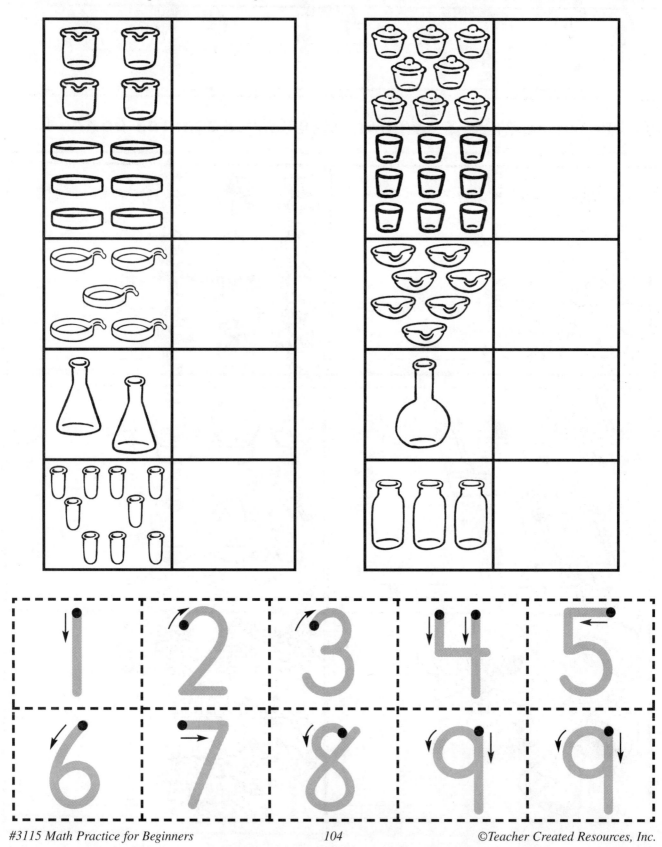

Name _____

Trace the numbers.

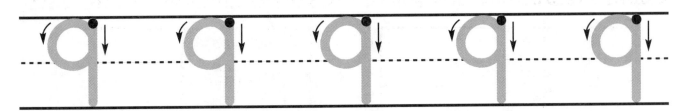

Write the number of animals in each box on the line.

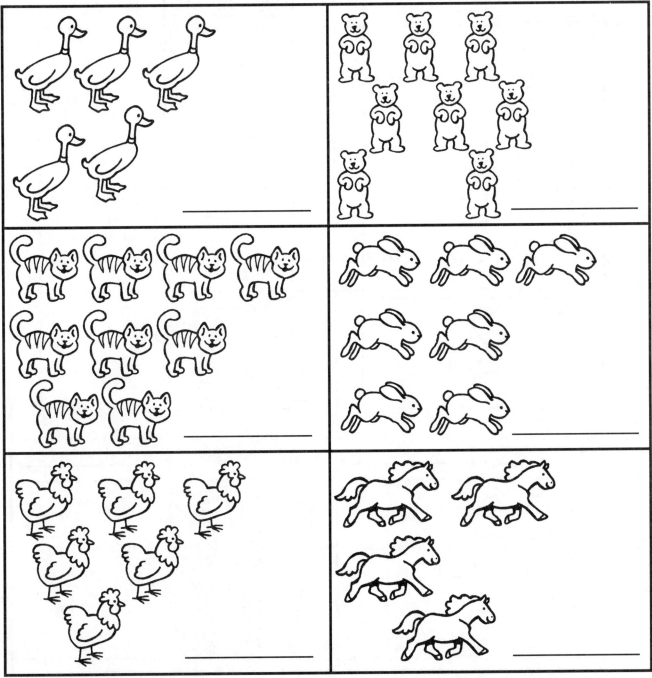

Name _____

Trace the numbers.

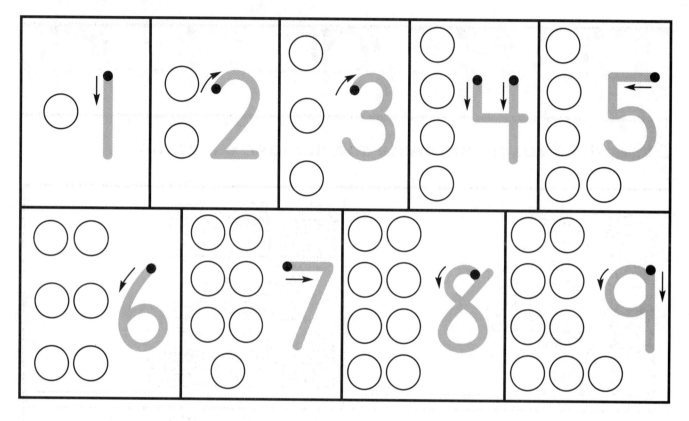

Count the fruits and write the number on the line.

106

Name _____

Trace the numbers.

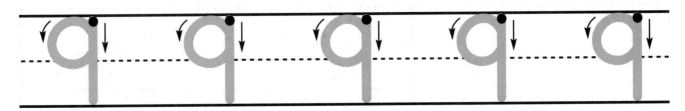

Count the houses and write the number on the line.

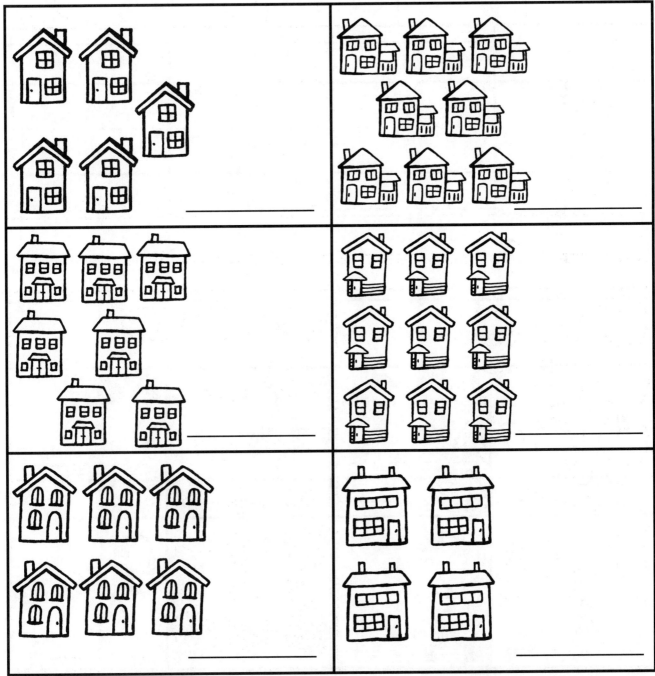

Name _____

Trace and write the numbers on the line.

Count the trees and write the number on the line.

Name _____

Trace and cut out the numbers at the bottom of the page.
Count the shapes and paste the correct number in the box.

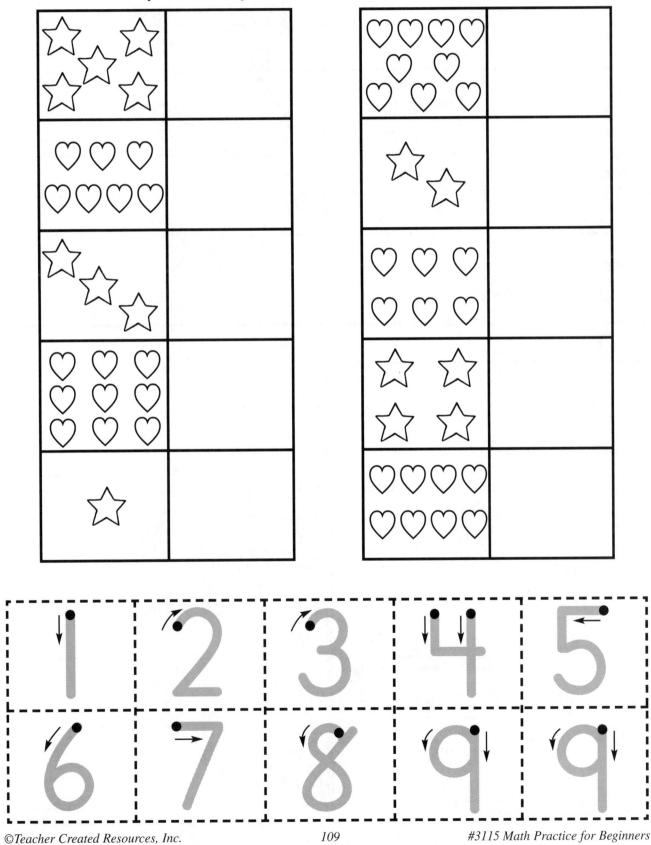

Name _____

Count the flowers and write the number on the line.

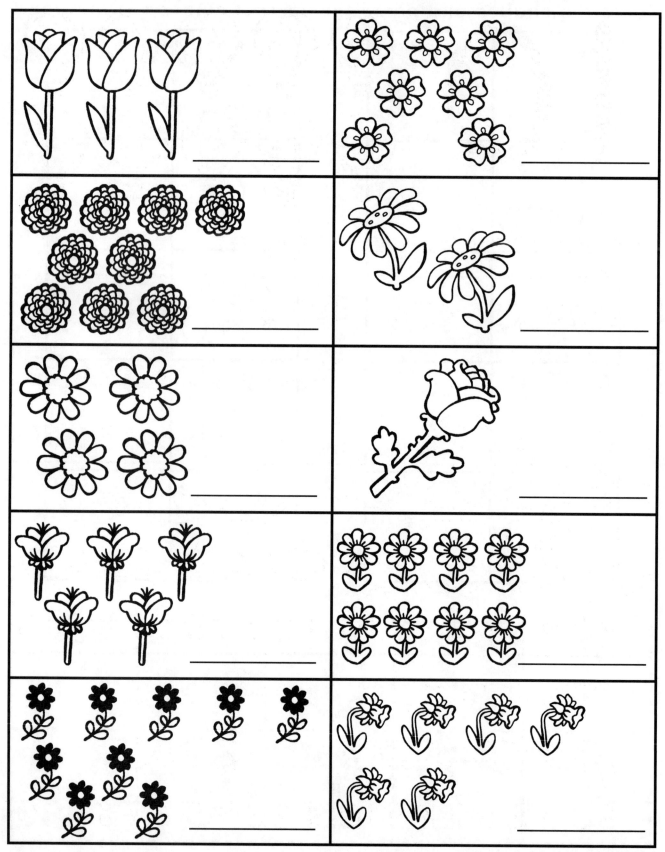

Name _____

Count ten hot air balloons.

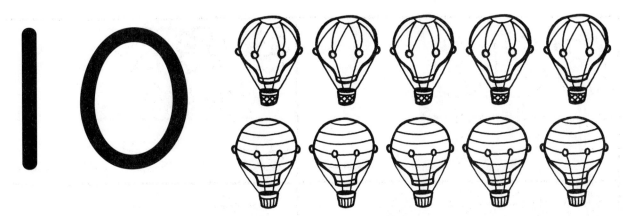

10

Circle the number of clouds in each box.

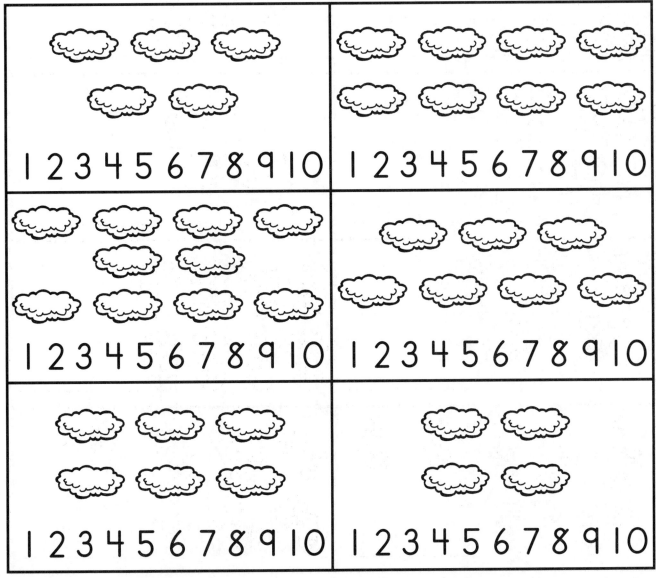

Practice writing the number ten.

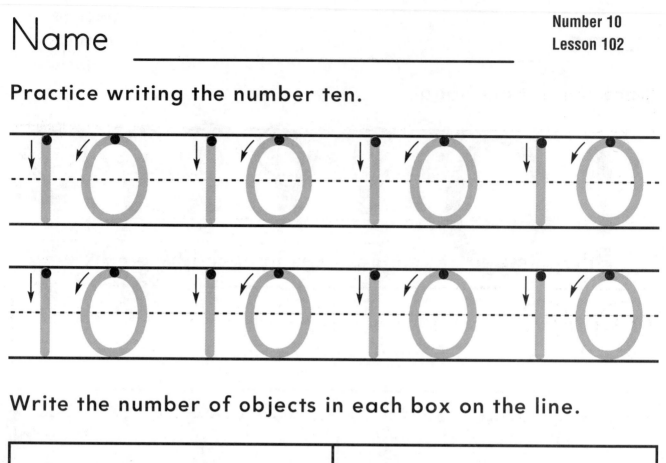

Write the number of objects in each box on the line.

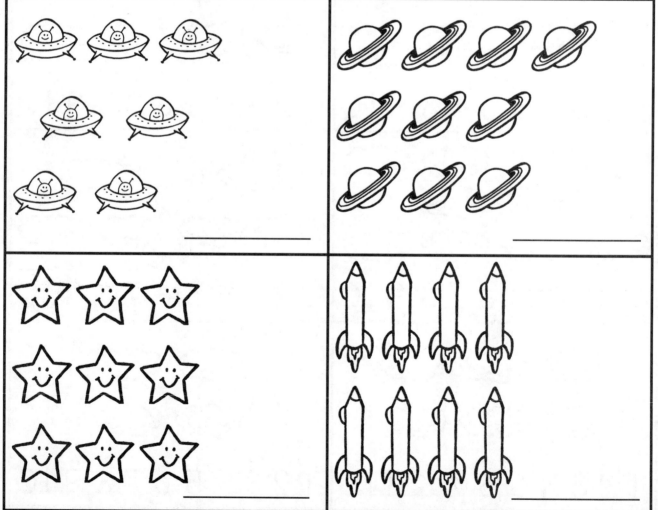

Name _____

Number 10
Lesson 103

Trace the numbers.

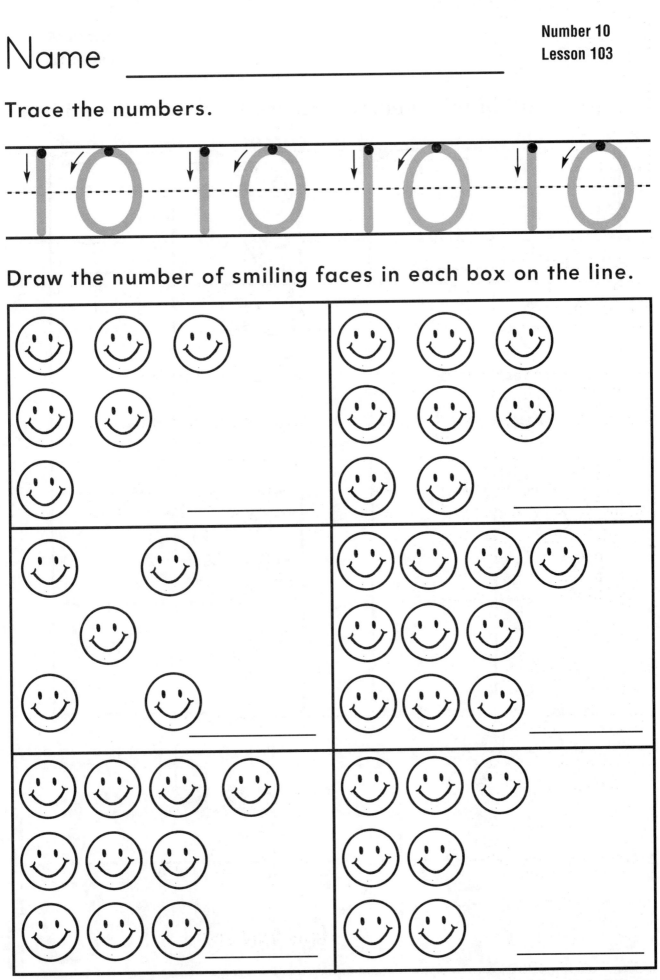

Draw the number of smiling faces in each box on the line.

©Teacher Created Resources, Inc.

113

#3115 Math Practice for Beginners

Trace and cut out the numbers at the bottom of the page.
Count the shapes and paste the correct number in the box.

Name

Trace the numbers.

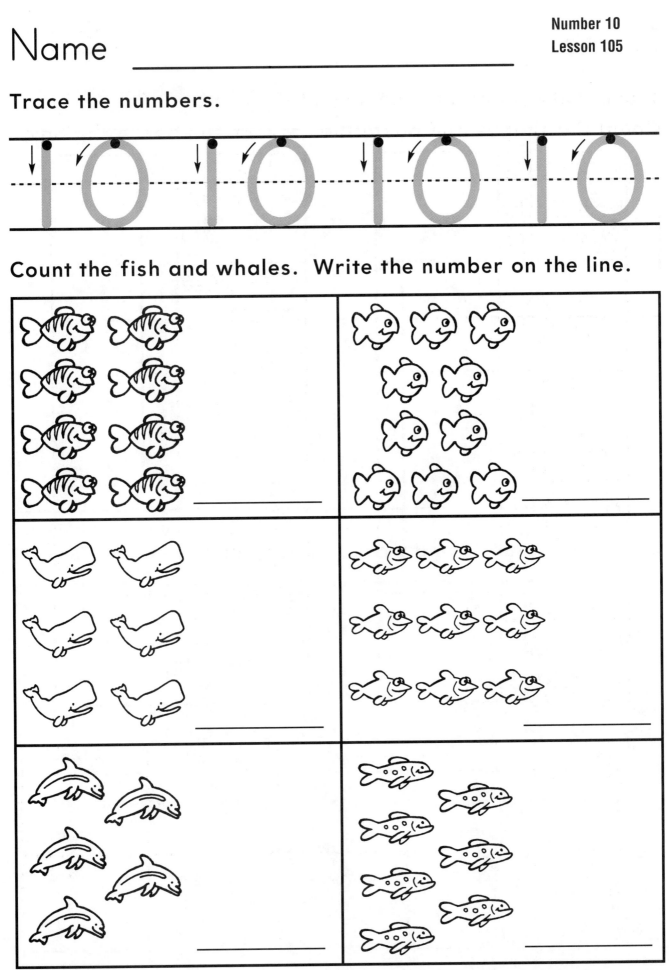

10 10 10 10 10 10

Count the fish and whales. Write the number on the line.

Name _____

Trace the numbers.

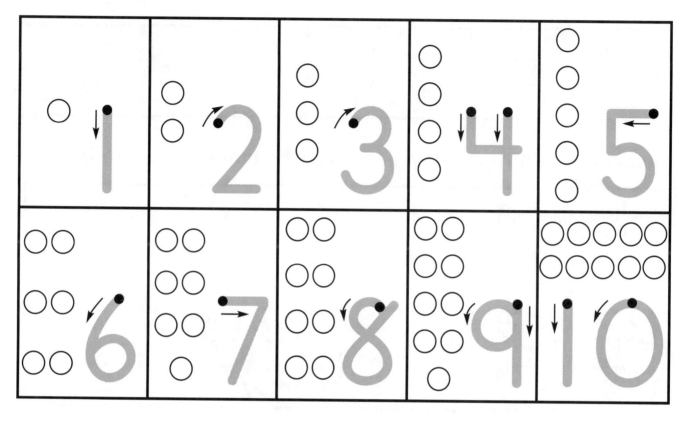

Count the desserts and write the number on the line.

Name _____

Trace the numbers.

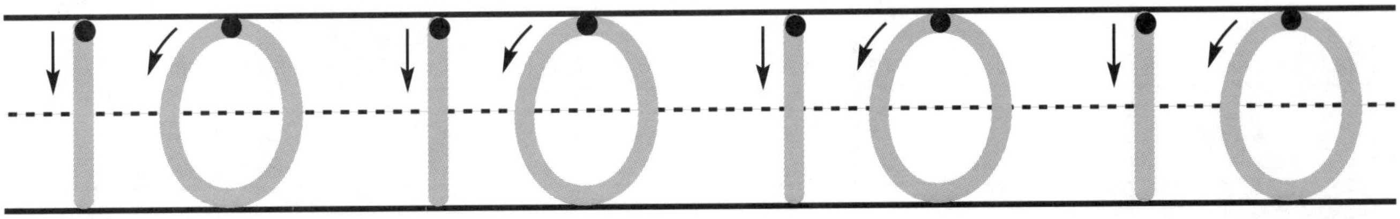

10 10 10 10 10

Count the animal faces and write the number on the line.

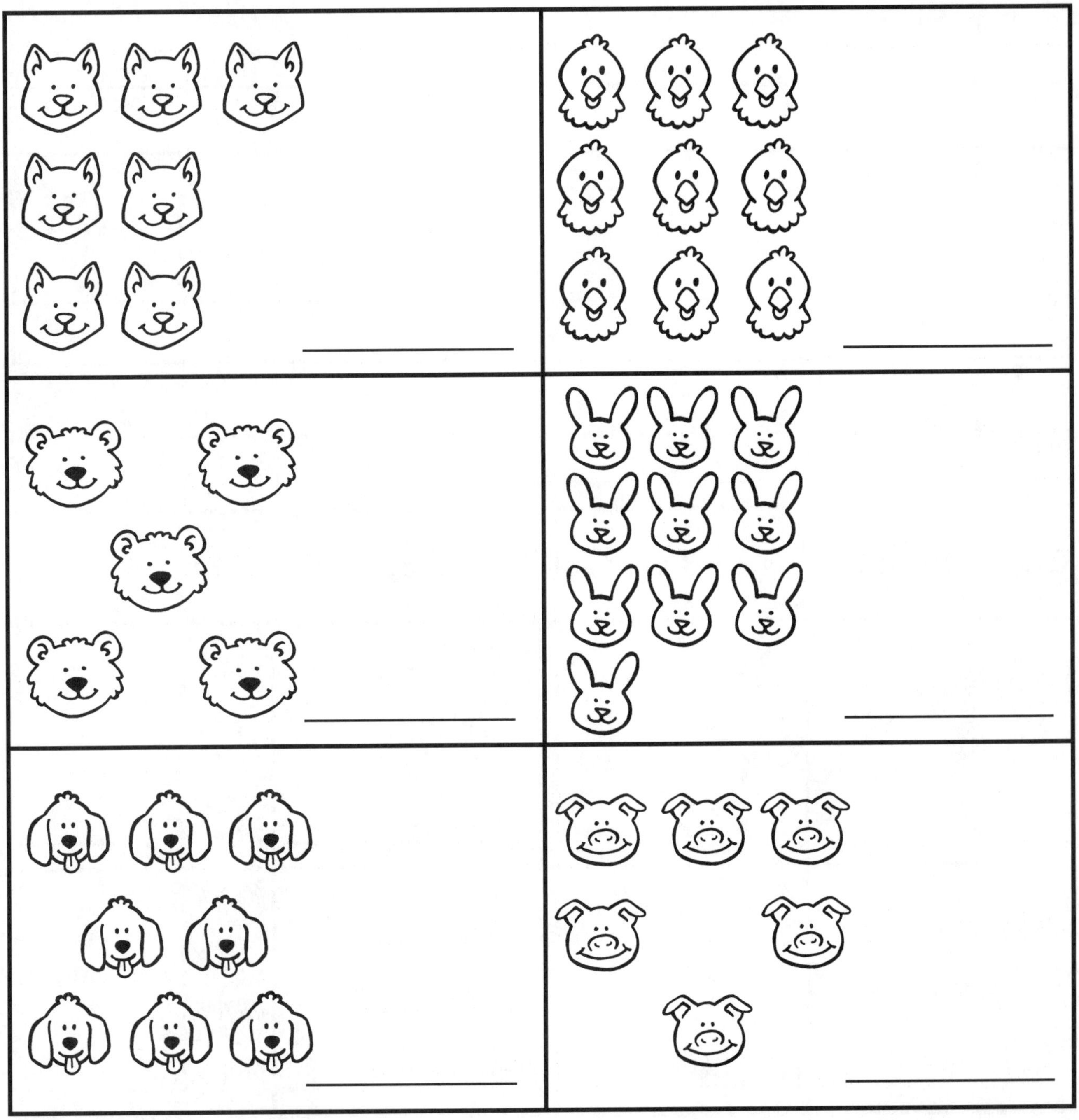

_____

_____

_____

_____

_____

_____

Name _____

Trace and write the numbers on the lines.

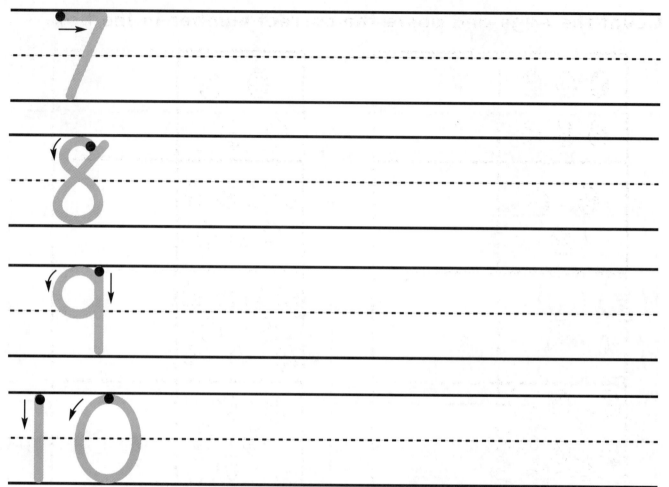

Count the buttons and write the number on the line.

Name _____

Trace and cut out the numbers at the bottom of the page.
Count the eggs and paste the correct number in the box.

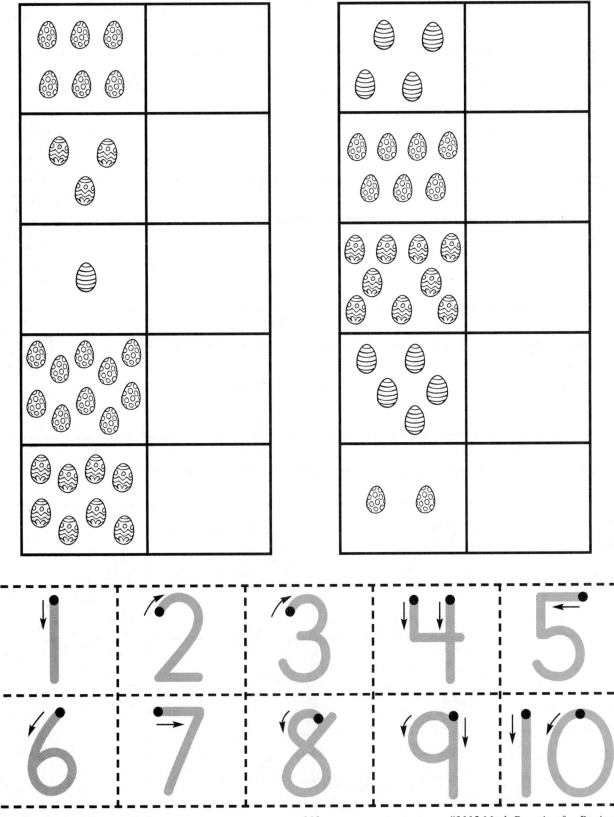

Name _____

Count the tools and write the number on the line.

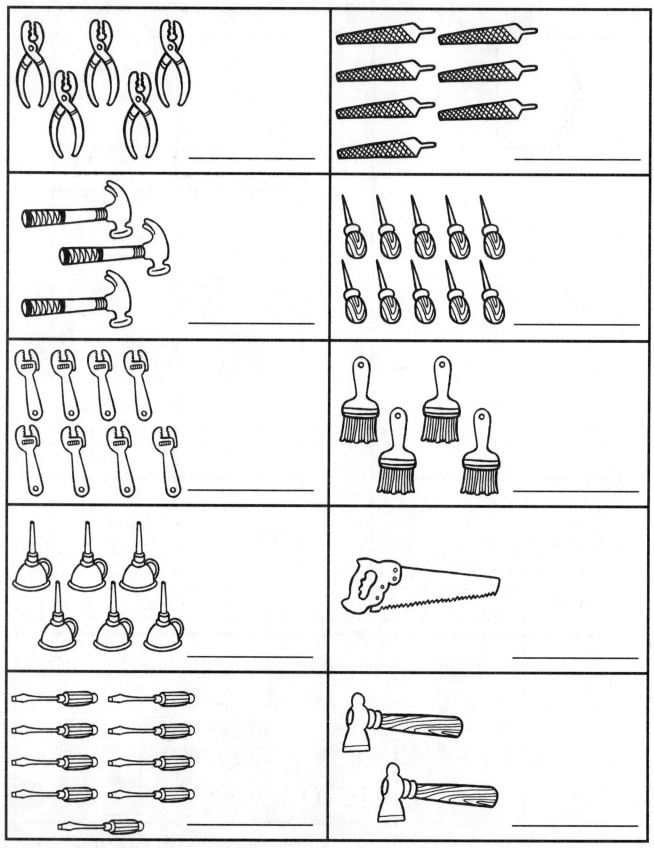

Name _____

There are no objects. There are zero objects.

Circle the number of vans in each box.

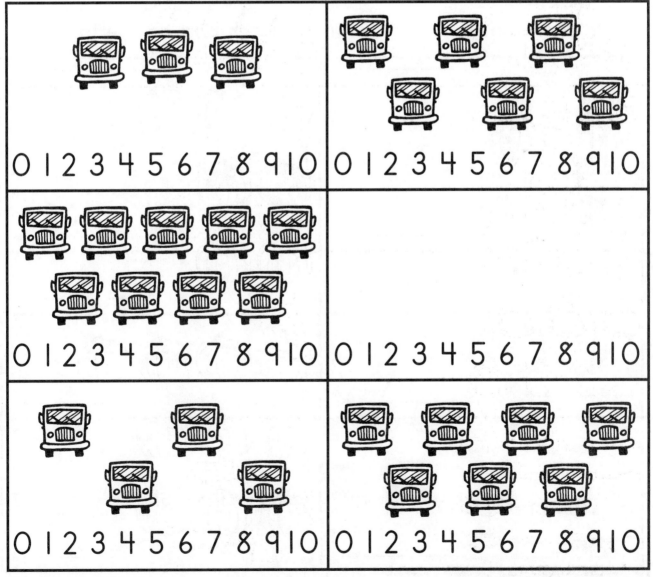

Practice writing the zeroes.

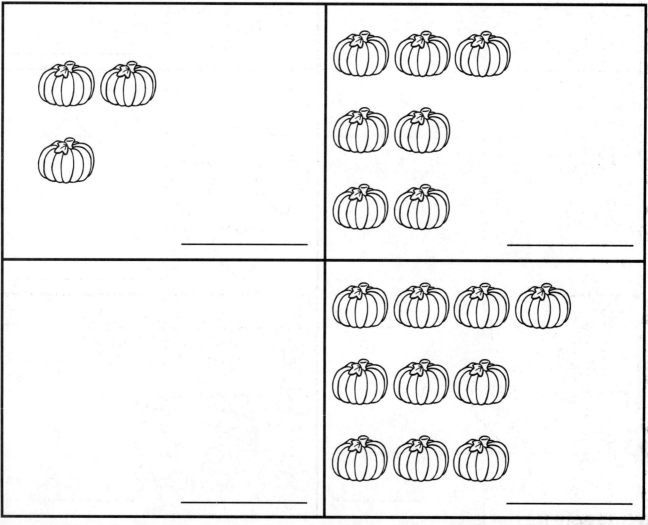

Write the number of pumpkins in each box on the line.

Name _____

Trace the numbers.

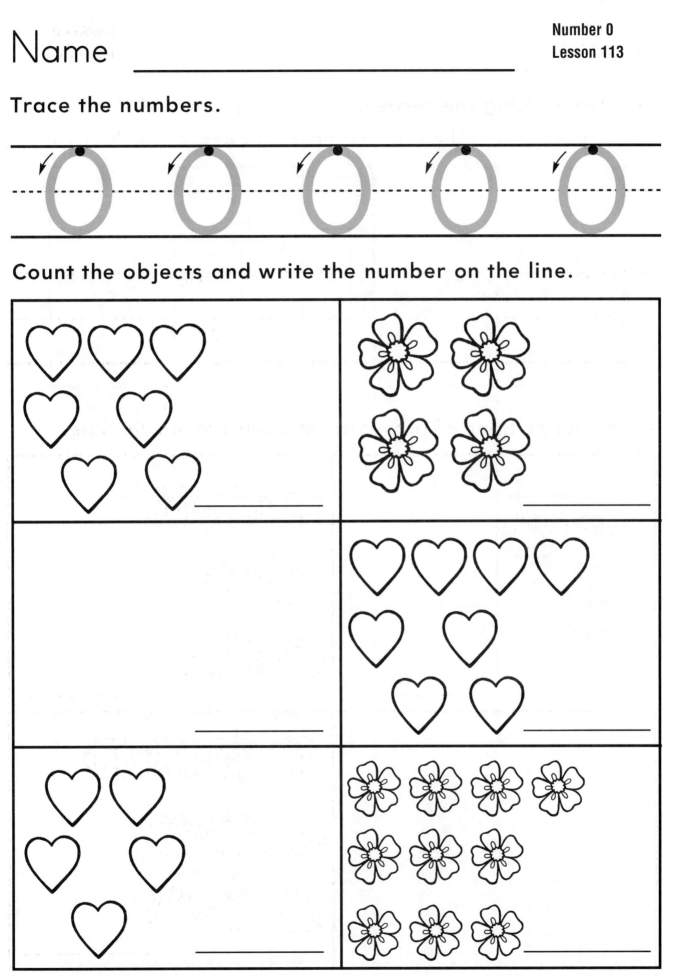

Count the objects and write the number on the line.

Name _____

Trace and cut out the numbers at the bottom of the page.
Count the kites and paste the correct number in the box.

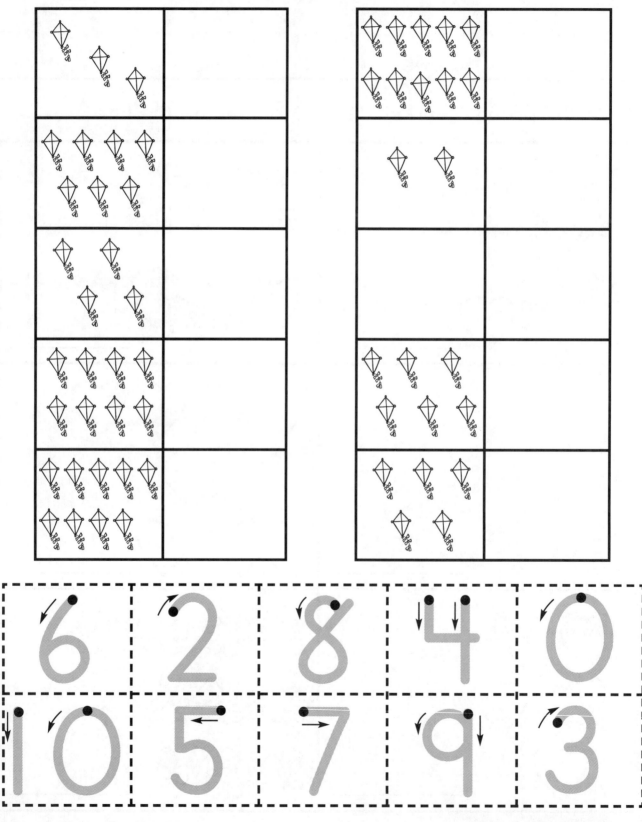

124

Name _____

Trace the number zero.

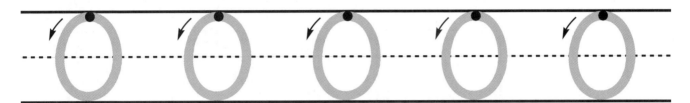

Write the number of faces in each box on the line.

Name _____

Trace the numbers.

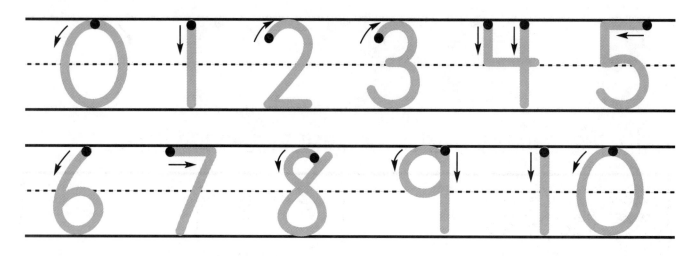

Write the number of balloons in each box on the line.

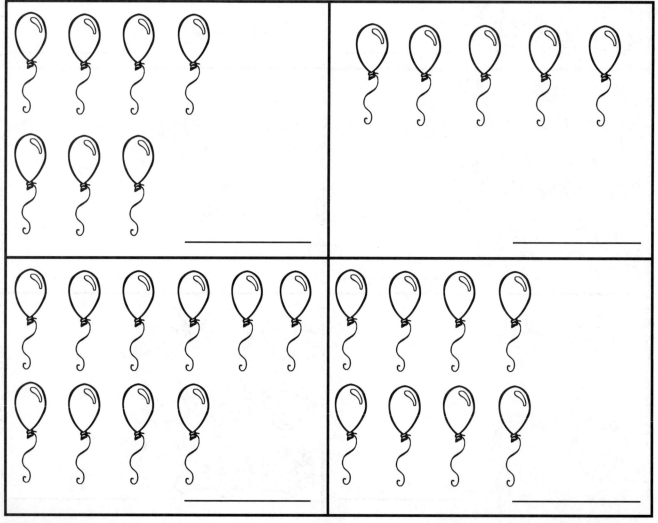

Name _____

Trace the number zero.

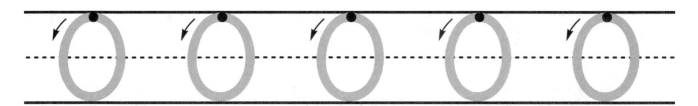

Count the animals and write the number on the line.

Trace and write the number zero on the lines.

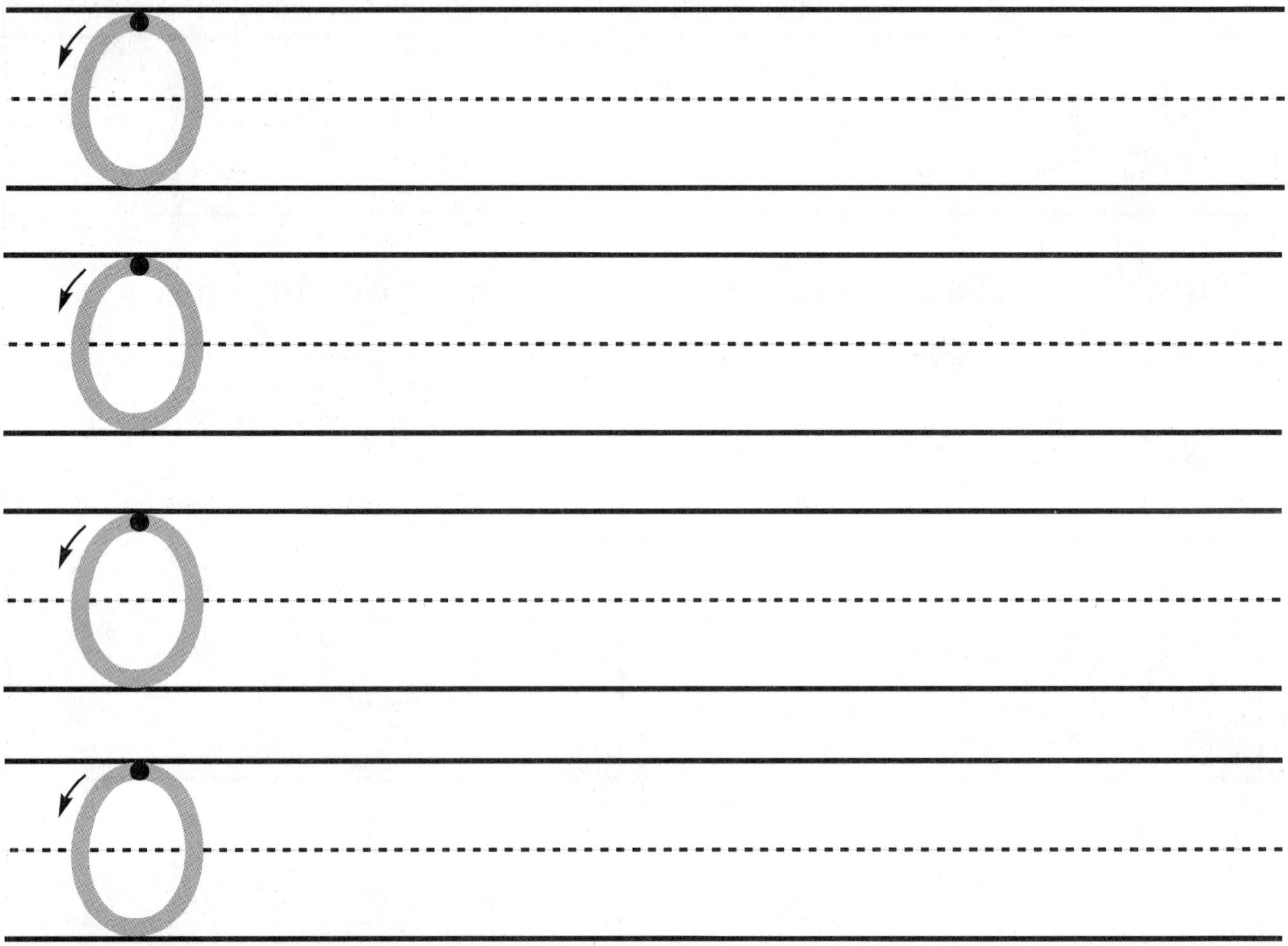

0

0

0

0

Count the elephants and peanuts in each box and write the number on the line.

Name _____

Trace and cut out the numbers at the bottom of the page.
Count the objects and paste the correct number in the box.

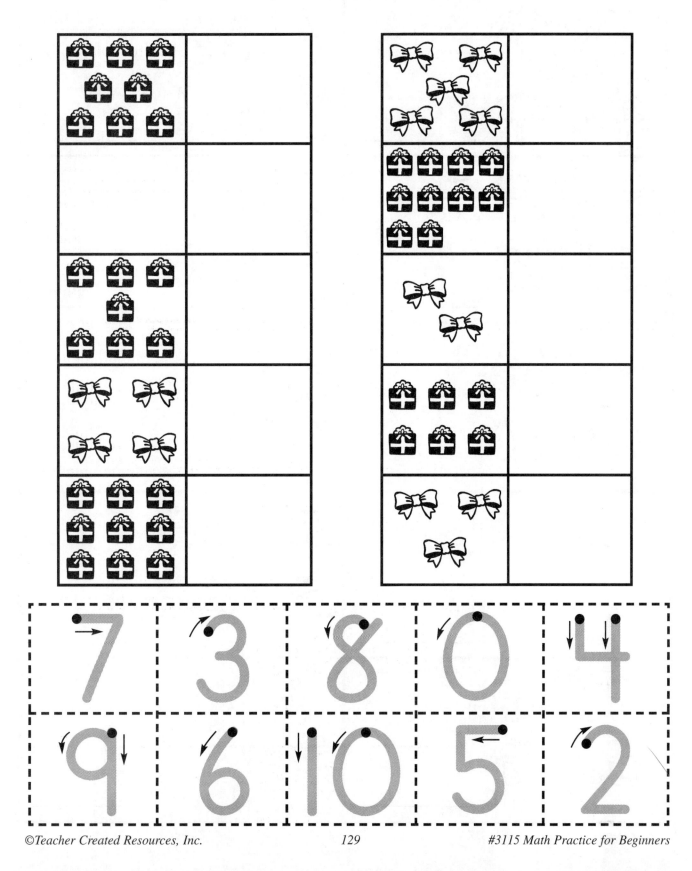

Name _____

Count the items. Write the number on the line.

Name Liberty

Color the pictures.
Write the total number in each box on the line.

Color 2 flowers red.

Color 1 flower purple.

3

_____

Color 1 cat black.

Color 3 cats orange.

_____

Color 2 balloons brown.

Color 2 balloons yellow.

_____

Color 1 car green.

Color 2 cars blue.

_____

Color 3 flags red.

Color 1 flag black.

_____

Name _____

Color the pictures.
Write the total number in each box on the line.

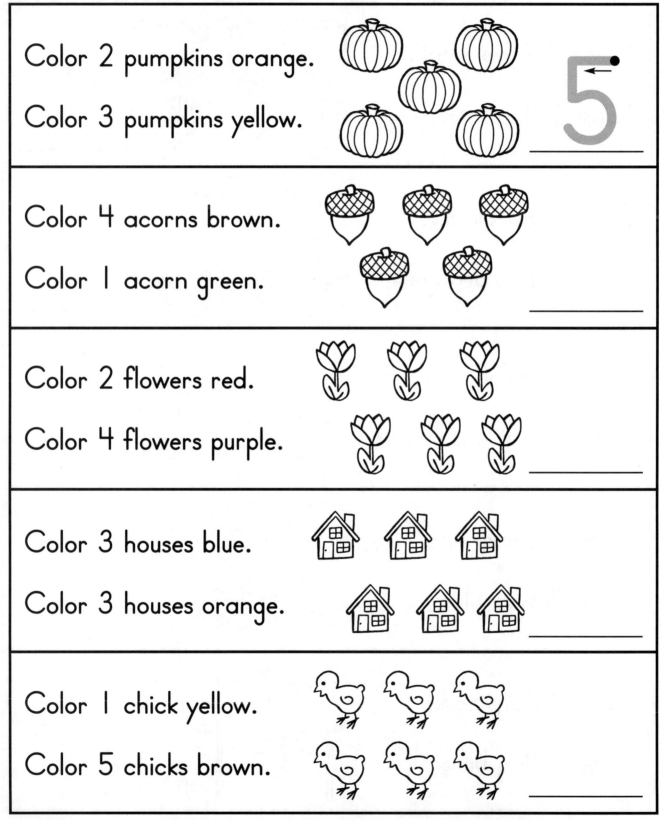

Color 2 pumpkins orange.

Color 3 pumpkins yellow.

5

_____

Color 4 acorns brown.

Color 1 acorn green.

_____

Color 2 flowers red.

Color 4 flowers purple.

_____

Color 3 houses blue.

Color 3 houses orange.

_____

Color 1 chick yellow.

Color 5 chicks brown.

_____

Name _____

Color the pictures.

Write the total number in each box on the line.

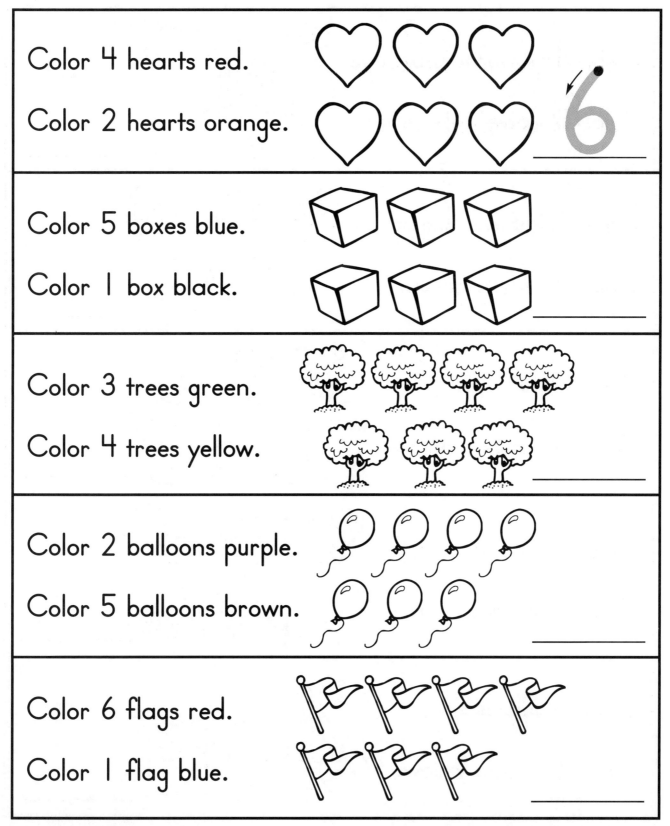

Color 4 hearts red.

Color 2 hearts orange.

Color 5 boxes blue.

Color 1 box black.

Color 3 trees green.

Color 4 trees yellow.

Color 2 balloons purple.

Color 5 balloons brown.

Color 6 flags red.

Color 1 flag blue.

Name _____

Color the pictures.

Write the total number in each box on the line.

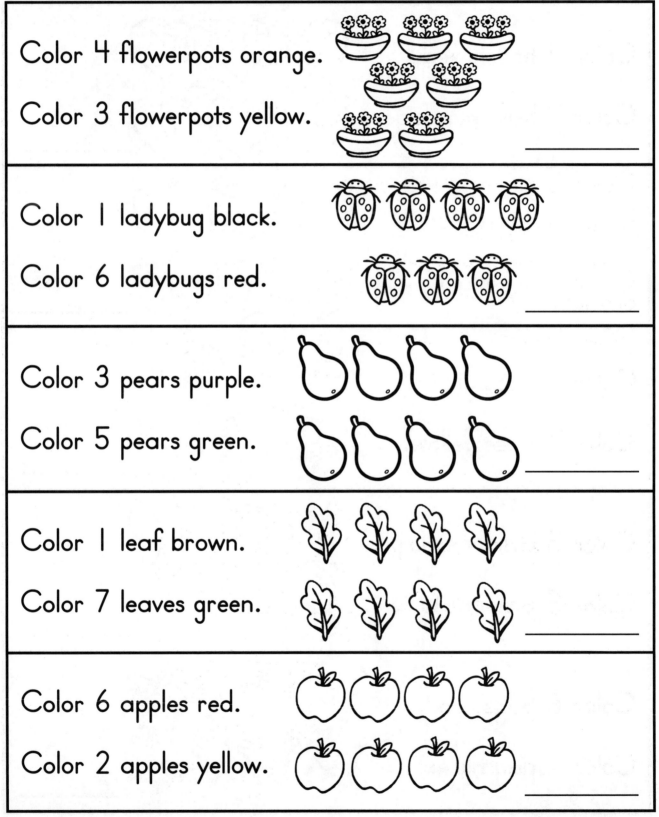

Color 4 flowerpots orange.

Color 3 flowerpots yellow. _____

Color 1 ladybug black.

Color 6 ladybugs red. _____

Color 3 pears purple.

Color 5 pears green. _____

Color 1 leaf brown.

Color 7 leaves green. _____

Color 6 apples red.

Color 2 apples yellow. _____

Name _____

Color the pictures.
Write the total number in each box on the line.

Color 4 balls green.

Color 4 balls purple.

_____

Color 5 gingerbread men brown.

Color 4 gingerbread men orange.

_____

Color 1 duck black.

Color 8 ducks yellow.

_____

Color 5 stars orange.

Color 5 stars blue.

_____

Color 9 pizzas red.

Color 1 pizza green.

_____

Name _____

Color the pictures. Write the total number on the line.

Color 2 flowers red.

Color 3 flowers orange.

2 and 3 is _____

Color 1 cat black.

Color 4 cats brown.

1 and 4 is _____

Color 2 gifts blue.

Color 2 gifts purple.

2 and 2 is _____

Color 1 car green.

Color 2 cars yellow.

1 and 2 is _____

Color the pictures. Write the total number on the line.

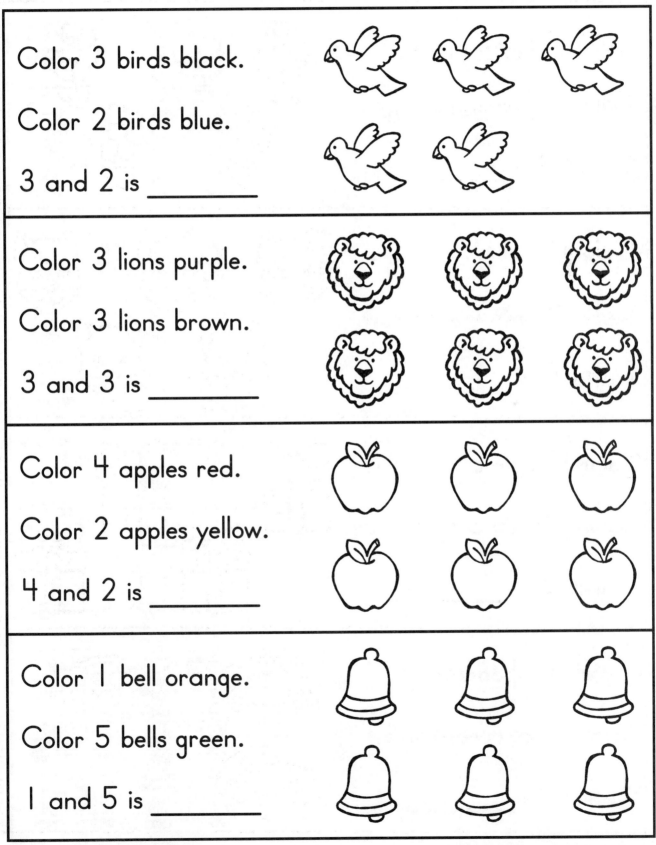

Color 3 birds black.

Color 2 birds blue.

3 and 2 is _____

Color 3 lions purple.

Color 3 lions brown.

3 and 3 is _____

Color 4 apples red.

Color 2 apples yellow.

4 and 2 is _____

Color 1 bell orange.

Color 5 bells green.

1 and 5 is _____

Name _____

Color the pictures. Write the total number on the line.

Color 3 engines blue.

Color 4 engines brown.

3 and 4 is _____

Color 1 train car purple.

Color 6 train cars yellow.

1 and 6 is _____

Color 5 train cars green.

Color 3 train cars orange.

5 and 3 is _____

Color 4 cabooses red.

Color 4 cabooses black.

4 and 4 is _____

Name _____

Color the pictures. Write the total number on the line.

Color 1 caterpillar green.

Color 7 caterpillars yellow.

1 and 7 is _____

Color 2 rabbits brown.

Color 6 rabbits blue.

2 and 6 is _____

Color 5 fish purple.

Color 4 fish red.

5 and 4 is _____

Color 6 chicks orange.

Color 3 chicks black.

6 and 3 is _____

Name _____

Color the pictures. Write the total number on the line.

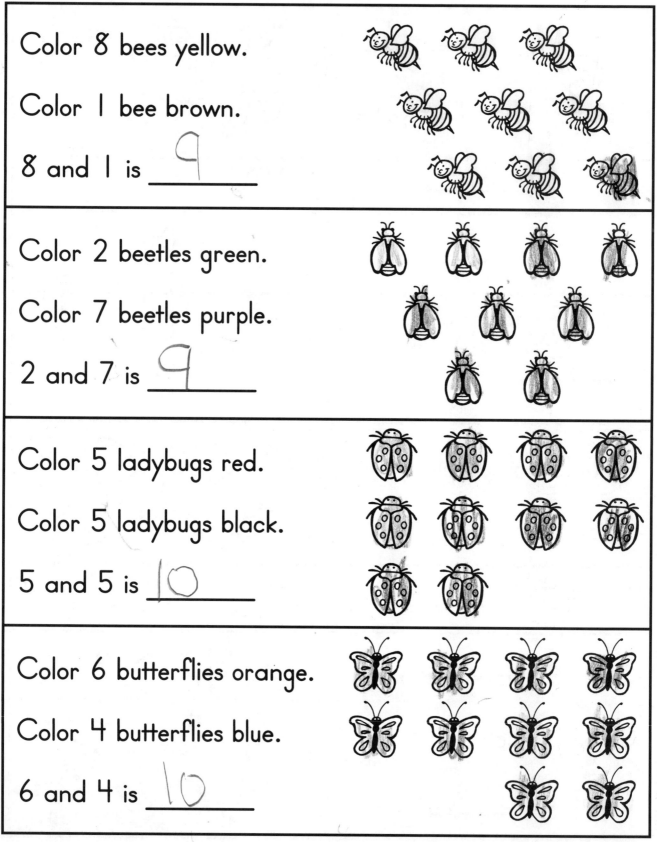

Color 8 bees yellow.

Color 1 bee brown.

8 and 1 is ___9___

Color 2 beetles green.

Color 7 beetles purple.

2 and 7 is ___9___

Color 5 ladybugs red.

Color 5 ladybugs black.

5 and 5 is ___10___

Color 6 butterflies orange.

Color 4 butterflies blue.

6 and 4 is ___10___

Name _____

Write the total number of circles in each box on the line.

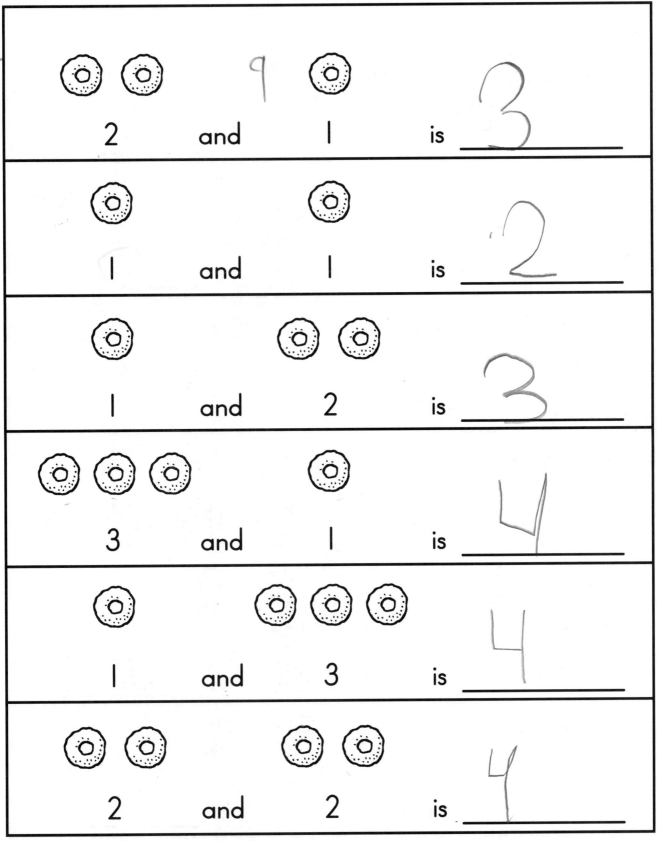

2   and   1   is   3

1   and   1   is   2

1   and   2   is   3

3   and   1   is   4

1   and   3   is   4

2   and   2   is   4

Name ______________________________

Addition Practice
Lesson 132

Write the total number of mice in each box on the line.

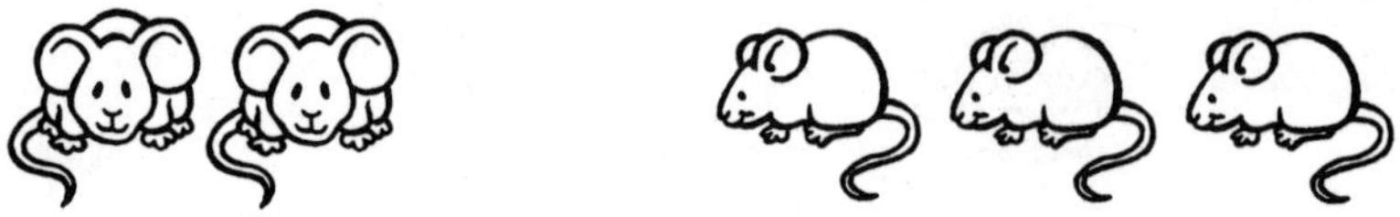

2 and 3 is ________

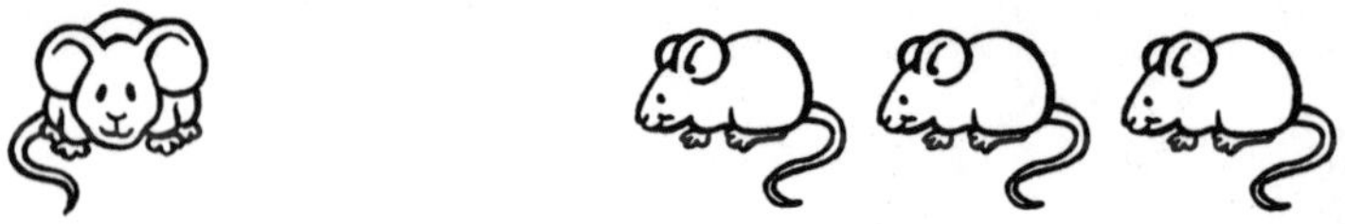

1 and 3 is ________

4 and 1 is ________

2 and 2 is ________

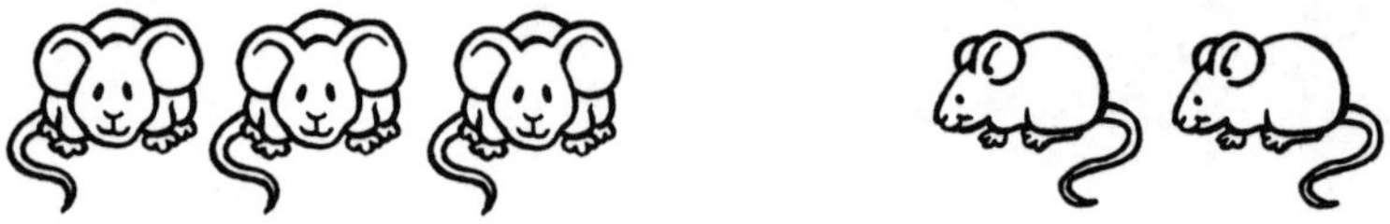

3 and 2 is ________

1 and 4 is ________

Name _____

Write the total number of turtles in each box on the line.

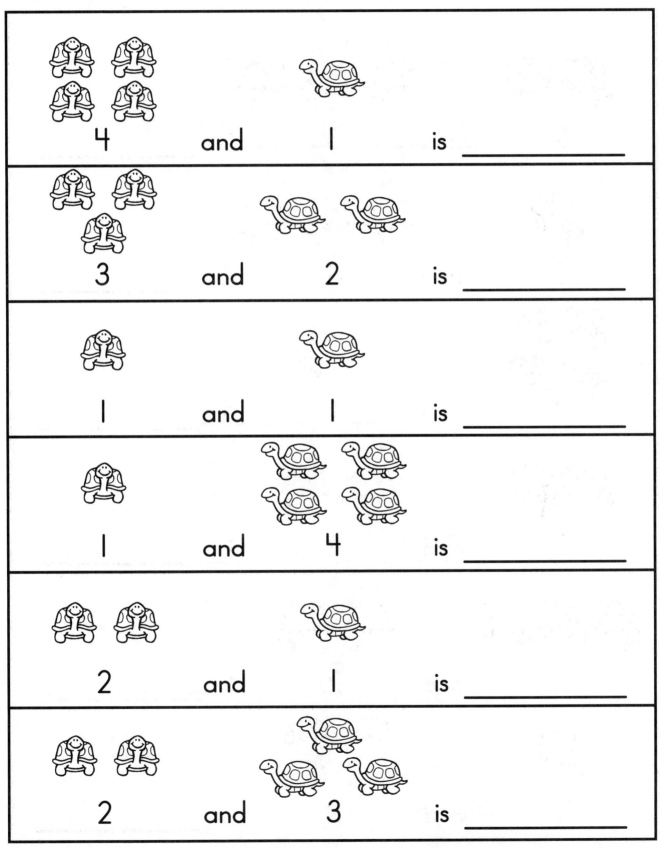

4   and   1   is _____

3   and   2   is _____

1   and   1   is _____

1   and   4   is _____

2   and   1   is _____

2   and   3   is _____

Name _____

Write the total number of sheep in each box on the line.

2   and   4   is _____

3   and   3   is _____

5   and   1   is _____

2   and   2   is _____

1   and   5   is _____

4   and   2   is _____

Write the total number of circles in each box on the line.

1   and   2   is _____

4   and   2   is _____

1   and   1   is _____

2   and   3   is _____

3   and   1   is _____

1   and   5   is _____

Name _____

Add the circles and write the total on the line.

2   and   2   is _____

1   and   2   is _____

3   and   2   is _____

1   and   3   is _____

4   and   1   is _____

2   and   3   is _____

Name _____

9

Add the cars and write the total on the line.

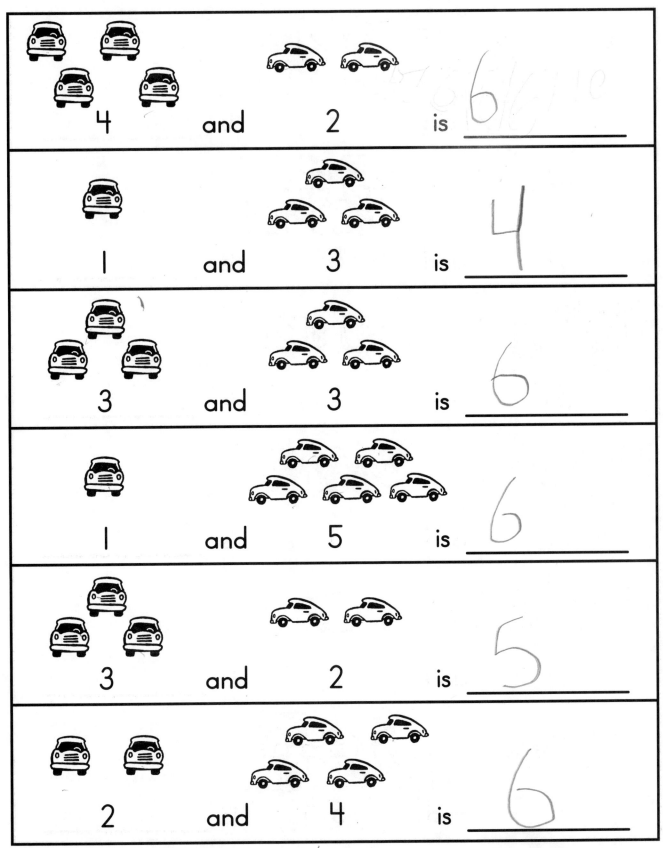

4 and 2 is 6

1 and 3 is 4

3 and 3 is 6

1 and 5 is 6

3 and 2 is 5

2 and 4 is 6

Name _____

Add the trucks and write the total on the line.

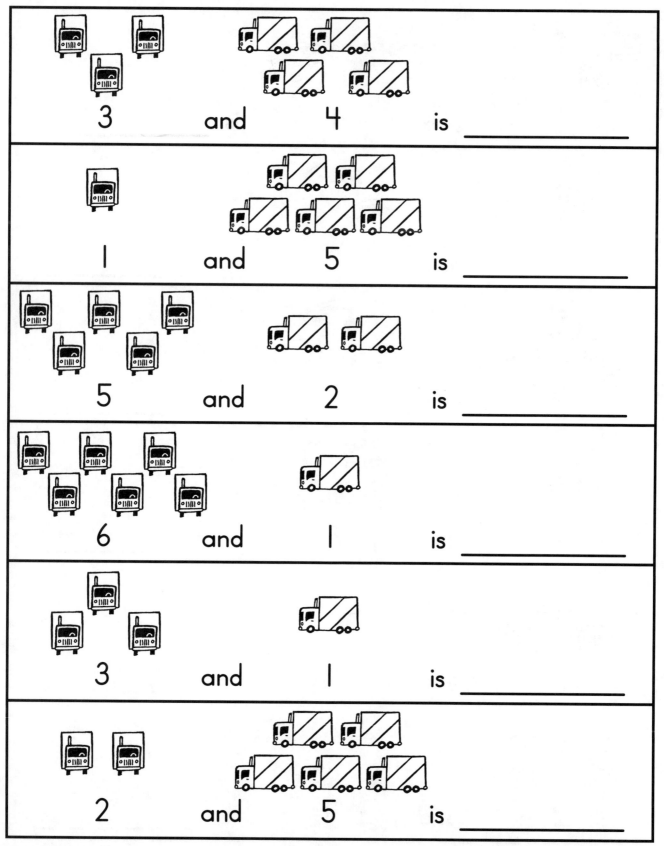

3 and 4 is _____

1 and 5 is _____

5 and 2 is _____

6 and 1 is _____

3 and 1 is _____

2 and 5 is _____

Name _____

Add the tricycles and write the total on the line.

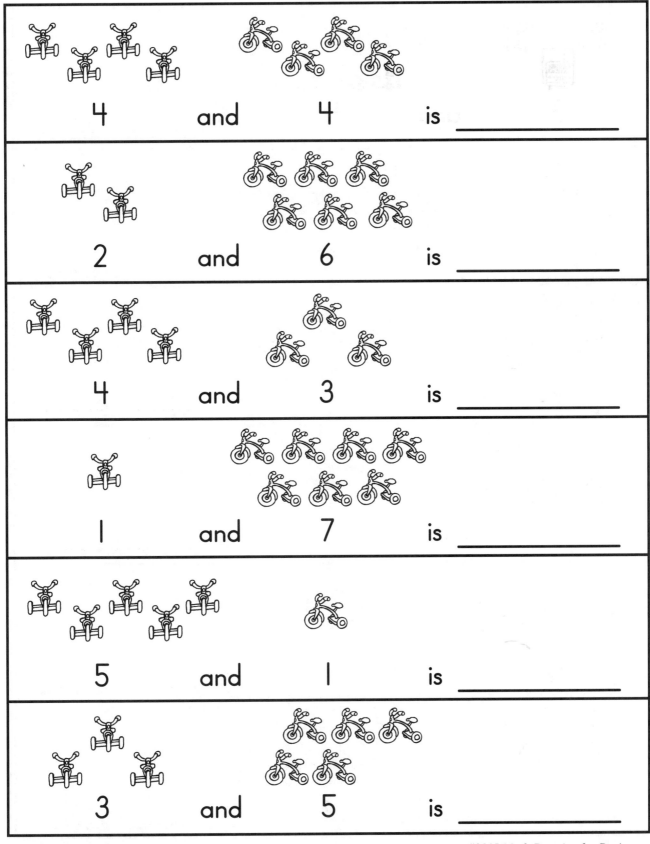

4   and   4   is _____

2   and   6   is _____

4   and   3   is _____

1   and   7   is _____

5   and   1   is _____

3   and   5   is _____

Name _____

Add the circles and write the total on the line.

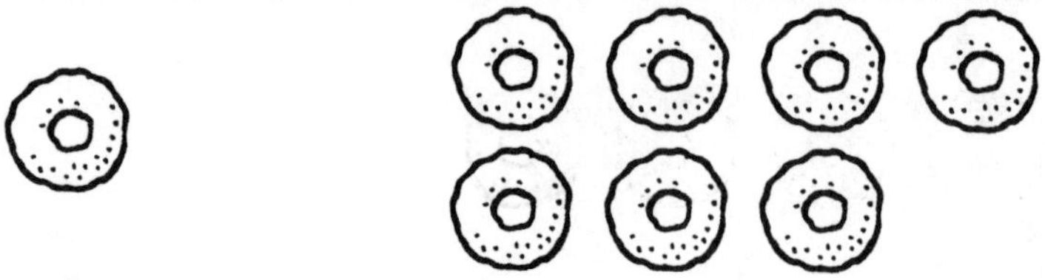

1 and 7 is _____

3 and 2 is _____

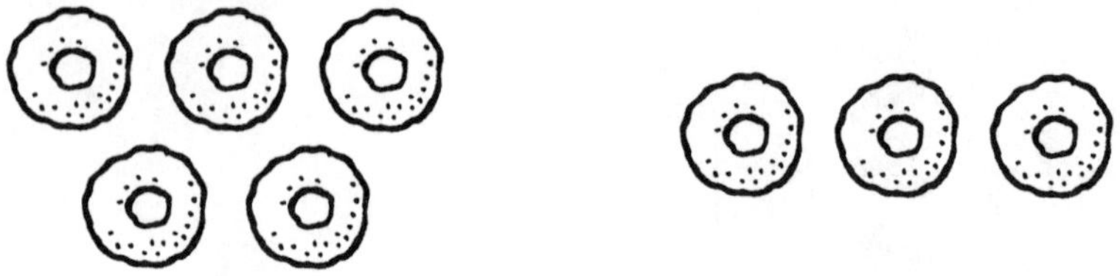

5 and 3 is _____

6 and 1 is _____

4 and 4 is _____

6 and 2 is _____

Name _____

Add the circles and write the total on the line.

3   plus   4   is _____

2   plus   3   is _____

6   plus   1   is _____

4   plus   2   is _____

2   plus   5   is _____

1   plus   4   is _____

Name _____

Add the bugs and write the total on the line.

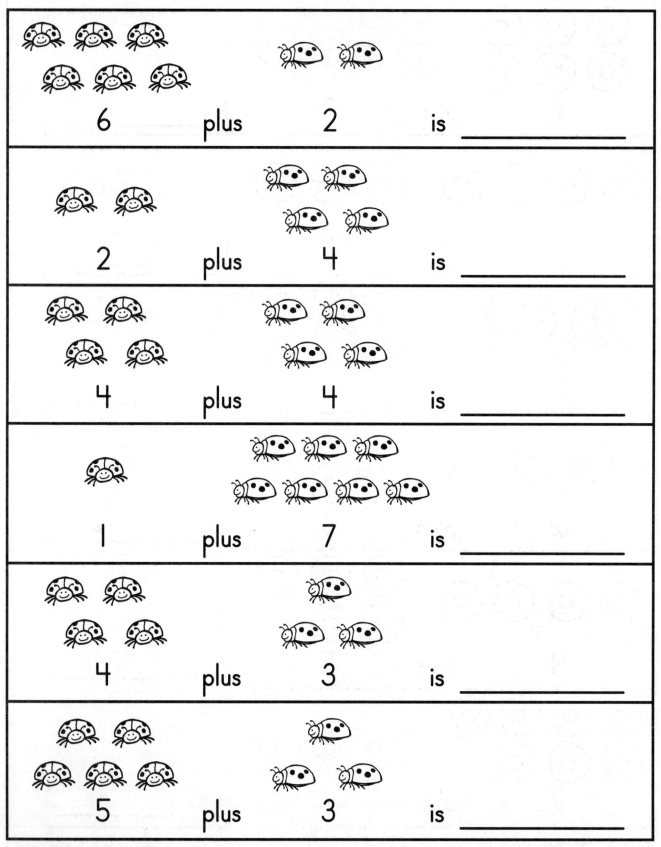

6   plus   2   is _____

2   plus   4   is _____

4   plus   4   is _____

1   plus   7   is _____

4   plus   3   is _____

5   plus   3   is _____

Name _____

Add the circles and write the total on the line.

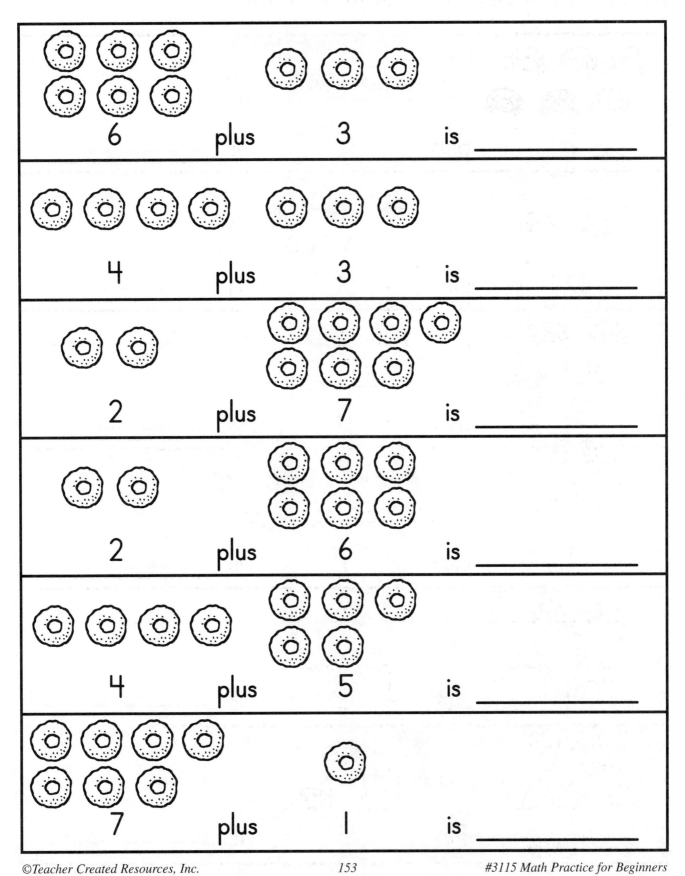

6   plus   3   is _____

4   plus   3   is _____

2   plus   7   is _____

2   plus   6   is _____

4   plus   5   is _____

7   plus   1   is _____

Name _____

Add the buses and write the total on the line.

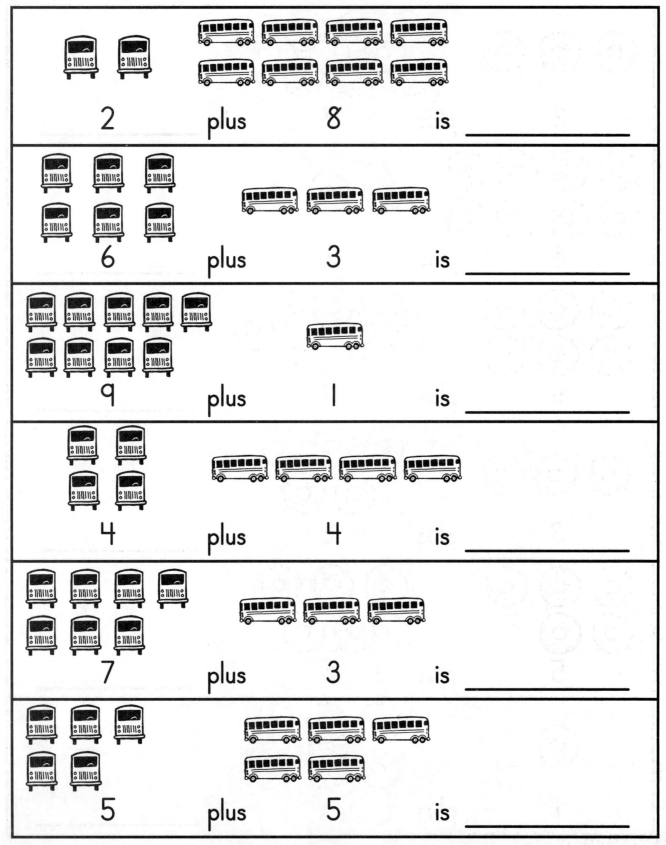

2   plus   8   is   _____

6   plus   3   is   _____

9   plus   1   is   _____

4   plus   4   is   _____

7   plus   3   is   _____

5   plus   5   is   _____

Add the circles and write the total on the line.

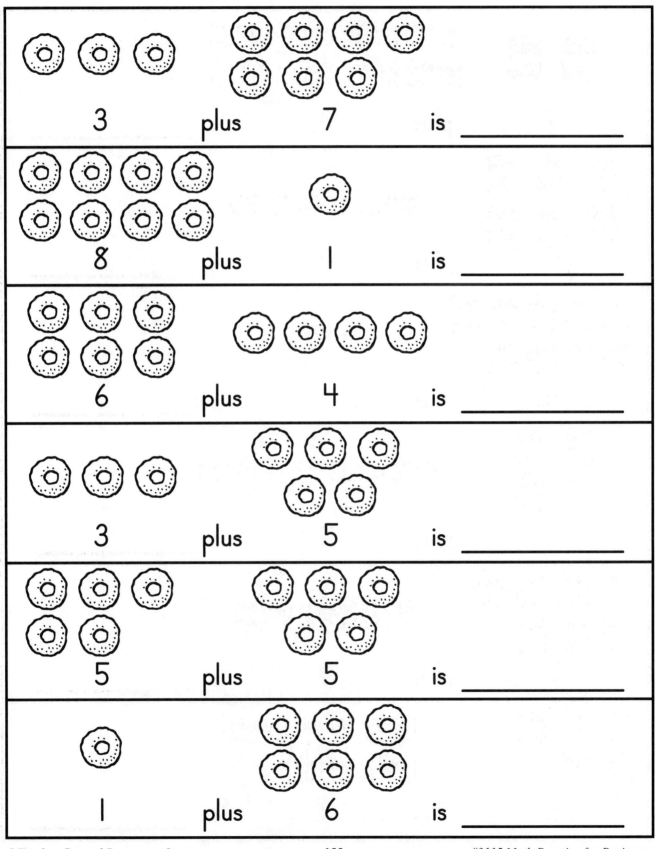

3   plus   7   is _____

8   plus   1   is _____

6   plus   4   is _____

3   plus   5   is _____

5   plus   5   is _____

1   plus   6   is _____

Name _____

Solve the problems.

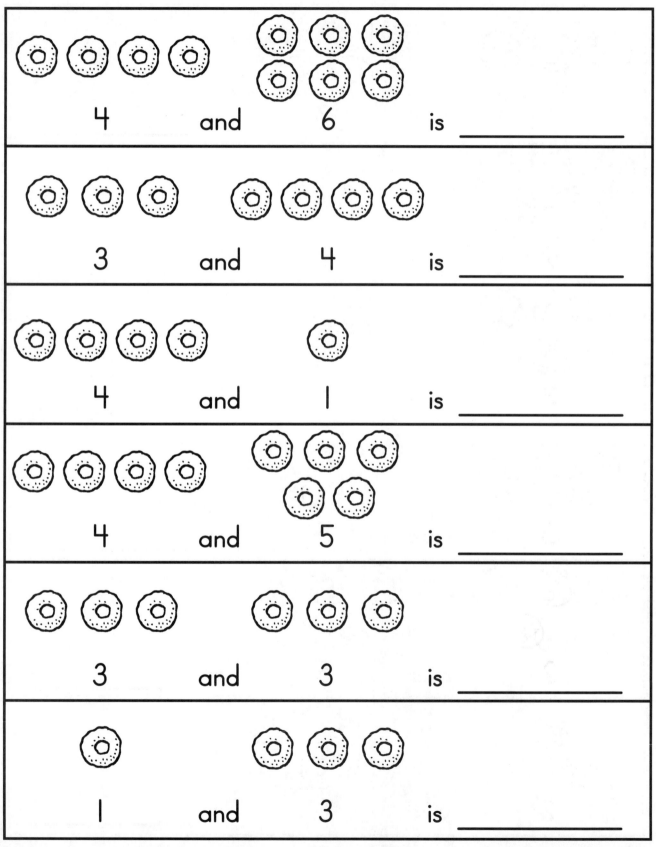

4   and   6   is _____

3   and   4   is _____

4   and   1   is _____

4   and   5   is _____

3   and   3   is _____

1   and   3   is _____

Name _____

Solve the problems.

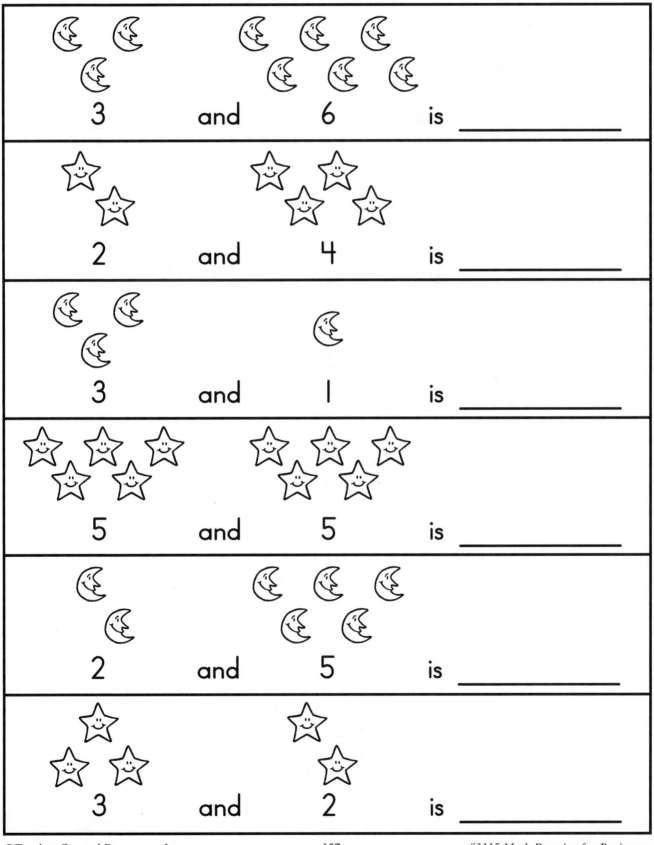

3   and   6   is _____

2   and   4   is _____

3   and   1   is _____

5   and   5   is _____

2   and   5   is _____

3   and   2   is _____

Name _____

Solve the problems.

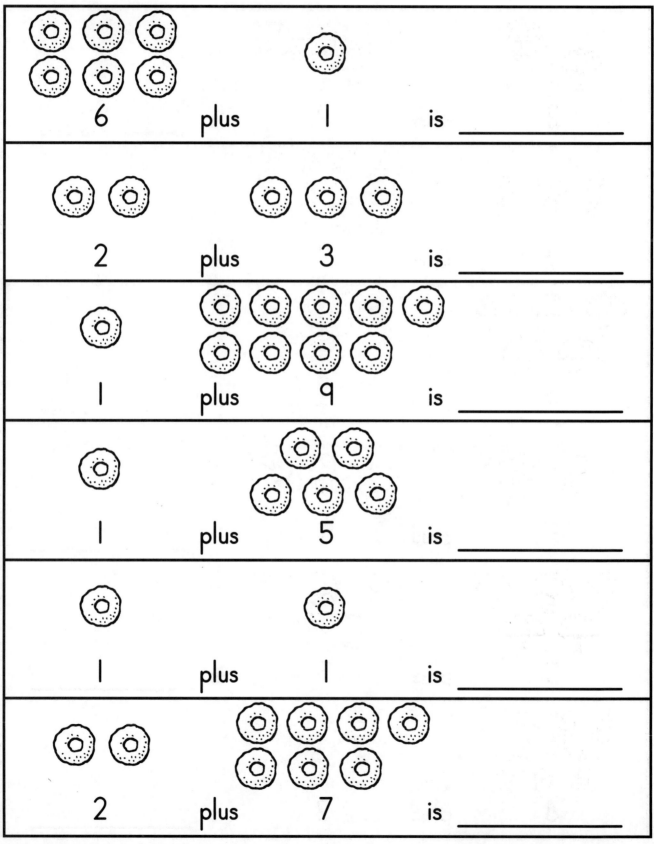

6   plus   1   is _____

2   plus   3   is _____

1   plus   9   is _____

1   plus   5   is _____

1   plus   1   is _____

2   plus   7   is _____

Name _____

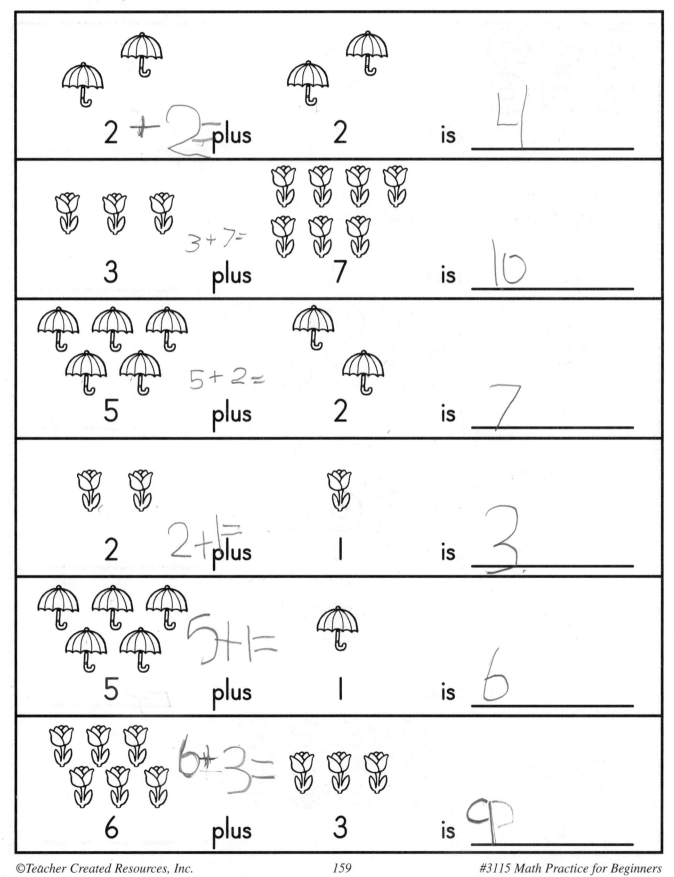

Solve the problems.

2 + 2 = plus 2 is 4

3 + 7 = 3 plus 7 is 10

5 + 2 = 5 plus 2 is 7

2 + 1 = 2 plus 1 is 3

5 + 1 = 5 plus 1 is 6

6 + 3 = 6 plus 3 is 9

Name _____

Solve the problems.

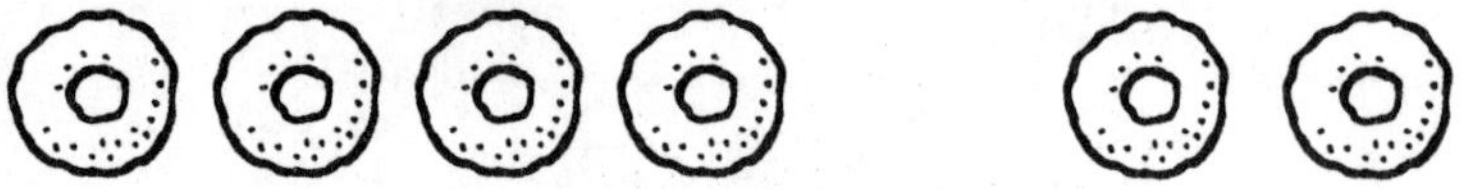

4   plus   2   is _____

1   plus   2   is _____

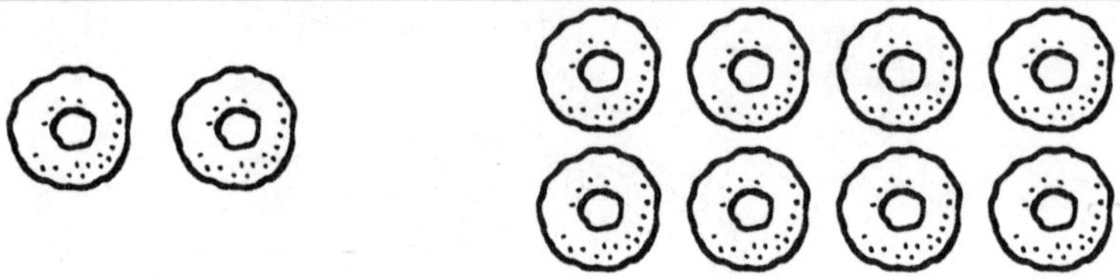

2   plus   8   is _____

4   plus   3   is _____

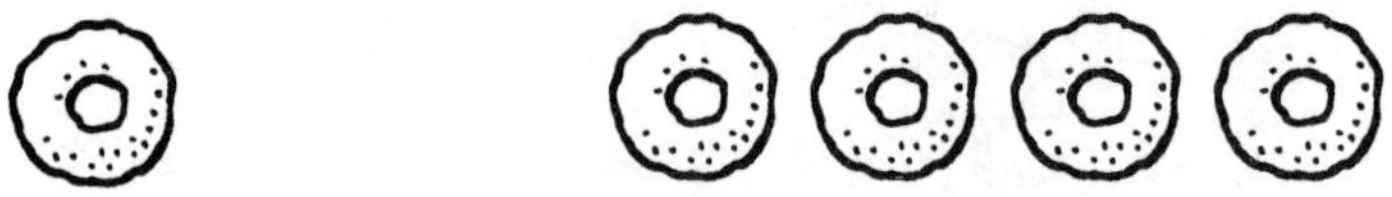

1   plus   4   is _____

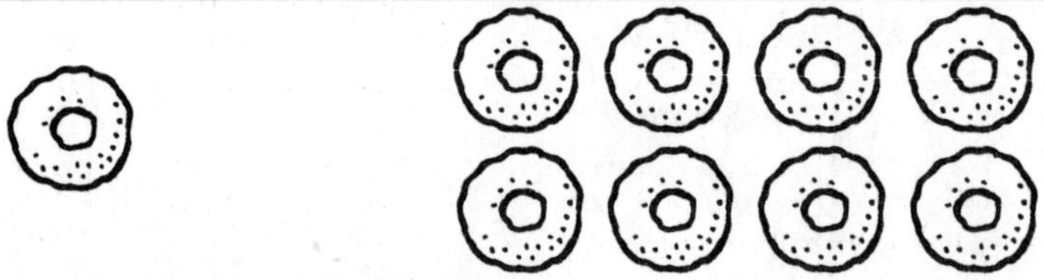

1   plus   8   is _____

Name _____

Color the objects. Cross out the number of objects to be subtracted. Write the number of objects left on the line.

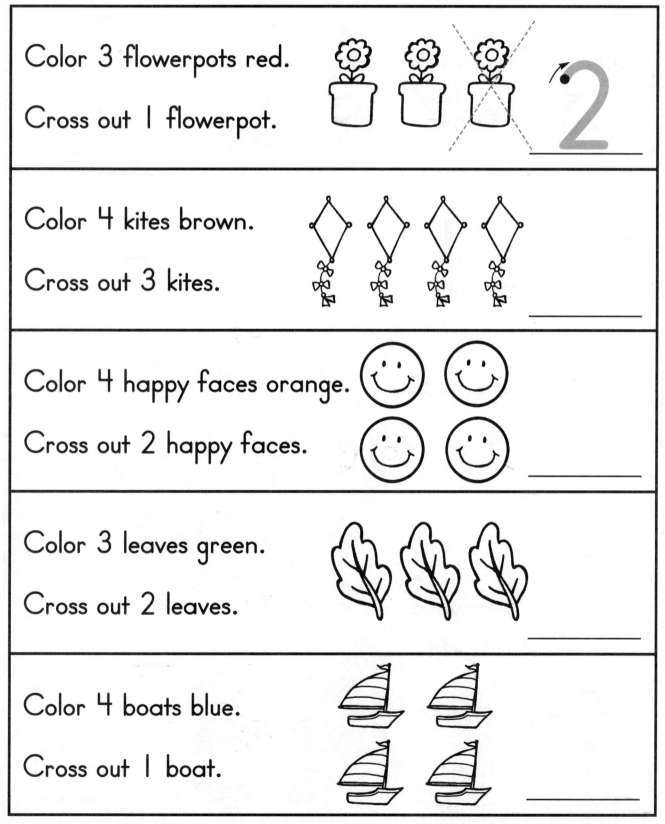

Color 3 flowerpots red.

Cross out 1 flowerpot.

Color 4 kites brown.

Cross out 3 kites.

Color 4 happy faces orange.

Cross out 2 happy faces.

Color 3 leaves green.

Cross out 2 leaves.

Color 4 boats blue.

Cross out 1 boat.

Name _____

Color the animals. Cross out the number of animals to be
subtracted.   Write the number of animals left on the line.

Color 5 fish orange.

Cross out 3 fish. 5 - 3 = 2

_____

Color 5 chicks yellow. 5 - 1 =

Cross out 1 chick.

_____

Color 6 bears purple.

Cross out 4 bears. 6 - 4 = 2

_____

Color 6 ladybugs red.

Cross out 3 ladybugs. 3 is

_____

Color 6 turtles green.

Cross out 1 turtle.

_____

Color the shapes. Cross out the number of shapes to be subtracted. Write the number of shapes left on the line.

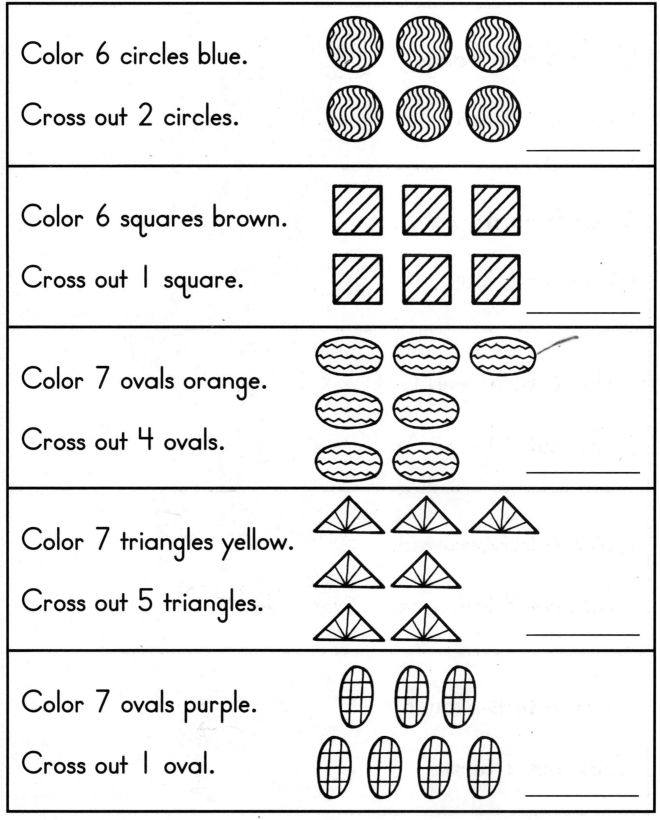

Color 6 circles blue.

Cross out 2 circles.

_____

Color 6 squares brown.

Cross out 1 square.

_____

Color 7 ovals orange.

Cross out 4 ovals.

_____

Color 7 triangles yellow.

Cross out 5 triangles.

_____

Color 7 ovals purple.

Cross out 1 oval.

_____

Color the balls. Cross out the number of balls to be subtracted. Write the number of balls left on the line.

Color 7 balls red.

Cross out 3 balls.

_____

Color 7 balls green.

Cross out 6 balls.

_____

Color 8 balls blue.

Cross out 5 balls.

_____

Color 8 balls brown.

Cross out 7 balls.

_____

Color 8 balls orange.

Cross out 2 balls.

_____

Name _____

Color the stars and circles. Cross out the number of objects to be subtracted. Write the number of objects left on the line.

Color 8 circles yellow.

Cross out 4 circles.

_____

Color 9 stars purple.

Cross out 4 stars.

_____

Color 9 circles red.

Cross out 8 circles.

_____

Color 10 stars green.

Cross out 5 stars.

_____

Color 10 circles blue.

Cross out 1 circle.

_____

Name _____

Color the pictures. Write the number left on the line.

Color 5 apples red.

Cross out 3 apples.

5 minus 3 is _____

Color 5 pears yellow.

Cross out 4 pears.

5 minus 4 is _____

Color 4 tomatoes blue.

Cross out 2 tomatoes.

4 minus 2 is _____

Color 3 melon green.

Cross out 1 melon.

3 minus 1 is _____

Name _____

Color the pictures. Write the number left on the line.

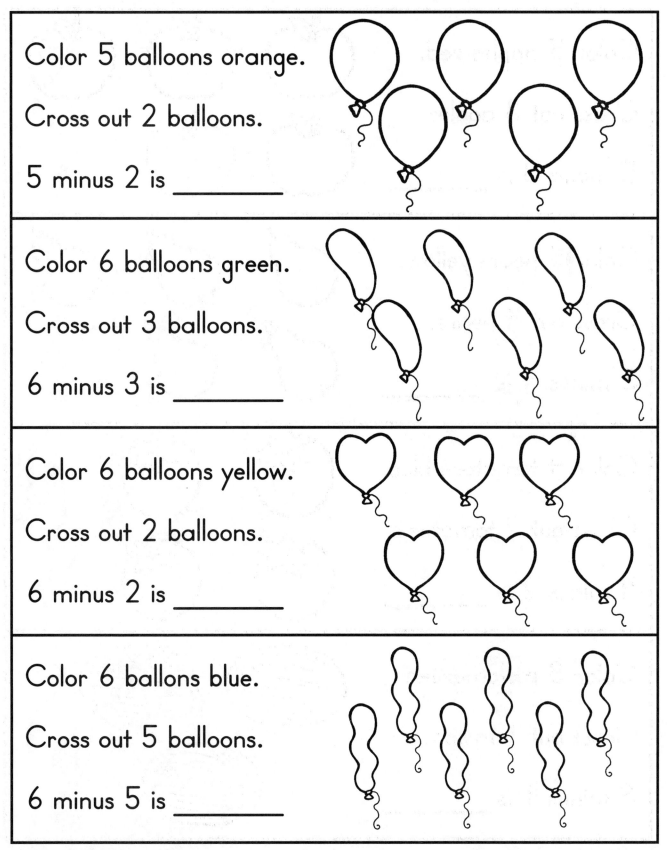

Color 5 balloons orange.

Cross out 2 balloons.

5 minus 2 is _____

Color 6 balloons green.

Cross out 3 balloons.

6 minus 3 is _____

Color 6 balloons yellow.

Cross out 2 balloons.

6 minus 2 is _____

Color 6 ballons blue.

Cross out 5 balloons.

6 minus 5 is _____

Name _____

Color the pictures. Write the number left on the line.

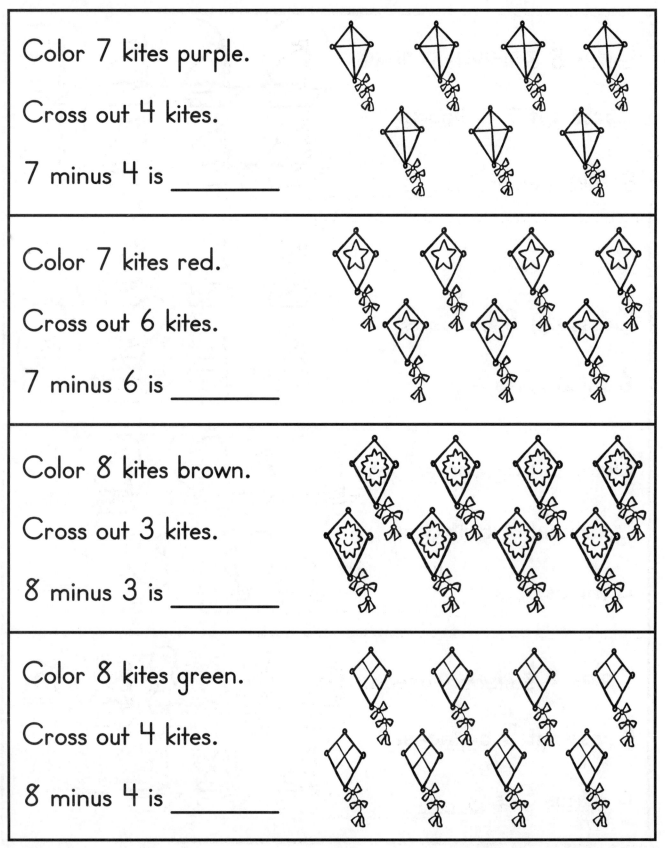

Color 7 kites purple.

Cross out 4 kites.

7 minus 4 is _____

Color 7 kites red.

Cross out 6 kites.

7 minus 6 is _____

Color 8 kites brown.

Cross out 3 kites.

8 minus 3 is _____

Color 8 kites green.

Cross out 4 kites.

8 minus 4 is _____

Name _____

Color the pictures. Write the number left on the line.

Color 8 sailboats yellow.

Cross out 7 sailboats.

8 take away 7 is _____

Color 8 sailboats red.

Cross out 6 sailboats.

8 take away 6 is _____

Color 9 sailboats blue.

Cross out 4 sailboats.

9 take away 4 is _____

Color 9 sailboats green.

Cross out 3 sailboats.

9 take away 3 is _____

Name _____

Color the pictures. Write the number left on the line.

Color 9 bears brown.

Cross out 1 bear.

9 take away 1 is _____

Color 9 cats orange.

Cross out 7 cats.

9 take away 7 is _____

Color 10 chicks blue.

Cross out 5 chicks.

10 take away 5 is _____

Color 10 ducks yellow.

Cross out 4 ducks.

10 take away 4 is _____

170

Name _____

Cross out the circles to be subtracted. Write the number left on the line.

3   take away   1   is   _____

2   take away   1   is   _____

3   take away   2   is   _____

4   take away   1   is   _____

4   take away   3   is   _____

4   take away   2   is   _____

Cross out the ladybugs and bees to be subtracted. Write the number left on the line.

5   take away   3   is _____

4   take away   3   is _____

4   take away   1   is _____

4   take away   2   is _____

5   take away   2   is _____

5   take away   4   is _____

Name _____

Cross out the circles to be subtracted. Write the number left on the line.

5   take away   1   is _____

5   take away   2   is _____

2   take away   1   is _____

5   take away   4   is _____

3   take away   1   is _____

5   take away   3   is _____

Name _____

Cross out the vehicles to be subtracted. Write the number left on the line.

6   take away   4   is _____

6   take away   3   is _____

6   take away   1   is _____

4   take away   2   is _____

6   take away   5   is _____

6   take away   2   is _____

Name _____

Cross out the circles to be subtracted. Write the number left on the line.

3   take away   2   is _____

6   take away   2   is _____

2   take away   1   is _____

5   take away   3   is _____

4   take away   1   is _____

6   take away   5   is _____

Name _____

Cross out the circles to be subtracted. Write the number
left on the line.

4   minus   2   is _____

3   minus   2   is _____

5   minus   2   is _____

4   minus   3   is _____

5   minus   1   is _____

5   minus   3   is _____

Name _____

Cross out the animals to be subtracted. Write the number left on the line.

6   minus   2   is _____

4   minus   3   is _____

6   minus   3   is _____

6   minus   5   is _____

5   minus   2   is _____

6   minus   4   is _____

Cross out the circles to be subtracted. Write the number left on the line.

7   minus   4   is _____

6   minus   5   is _____

7   minus   2   is _____

7   minus   1   is _____

4   minus   1   is _____

7   minus   5   is _____

Name _____

Cross out the animals to be subtracted. Write the number left on the line.

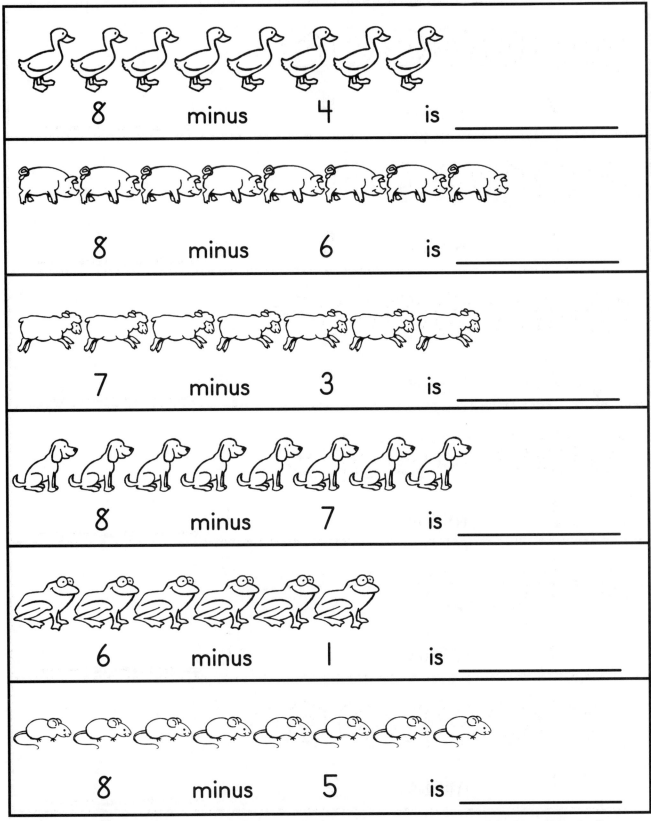

8   minus   4   is _____

8   minus   6   is _____

7   minus   3   is _____

8   minus   7   is _____

6   minus   1   is _____

8   minus   5   is _____

Cross out the circles to be subtracted. Write the number left on the line.

8   minus   7   is _____

5   minus   2   is _____

8   minus   3   is _____

7   minus   1   is _____

8   minus   4   is _____

8   minus   2   is _____

Name _____

Cross out the circles to be subtracted. Write the number left on the line.

7   take away   4   is _____

5   take away   3   is _____

7   take away   1   is _____

6   take away   2   is _____

7   take away   5   is _____

5   take away   4   is _____

Name _____

Cross out the suns, stars, and moons to be subtracted.
Write the number left on the line.

8   minus   2   is _____

6   minus   4   is _____

8   minus   4   is _____

8   minus   7   is _____

7   minus   3   is _____

8   minus   3   is _____

Name _____

Cross out the circles to be subtracted. Write the number left on the line.

9   minus   2   is _____

7   minus   3   is _____

9   minus   7   is _____

8   minus   6   is _____

9   minus   5   is _____

8   minus   1   is _____

Name _____

Cross out the desserts to be subtracted. Write the number left on the line.

10   take away   8   is _____

9   take away   3   is _____

10   take away   1   is _____

8   take away   4   is _____

10   take away   3   is _____

10   take away   5   is _____

     184   ©*Teacher Created Resources, Inc.*

Name _____

Cross out the circles to be subtracted. Write the number left on the line.

◎ ◎ ◎ ◎ ◎ ◎ ◎ ◎ ◎ ◎

10   minus   7   is _____

◎ ◎ ◎ ◎ ◎ ◎ ◎ ◎ ◎

9   minus   1   is _____

◎ ◎ ◎ ◎ ◎ ◎ ◎ ◎ ◎ ◎

10   minus   4   is _____

◎ ◎ ◎ ◎ ◎ ◎ ◎ ◎

8   minus   5   is _____

◎ ◎ ◎ ◎ ◎ ◎ ◎ ◎ ◎ ◎

10   minus   5   is _____

◎ ◎ ◎ ◎ ◎ ◎ ◎

7   minus   6   is _____

Name ______________________

Subtraction Practice
Lesson 176

Solve the problems.

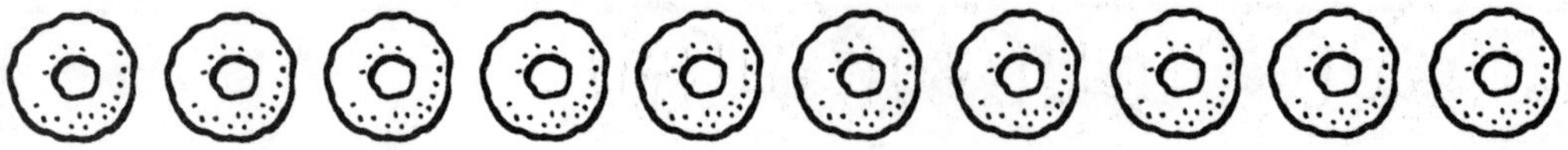

10 minus 6 is ______

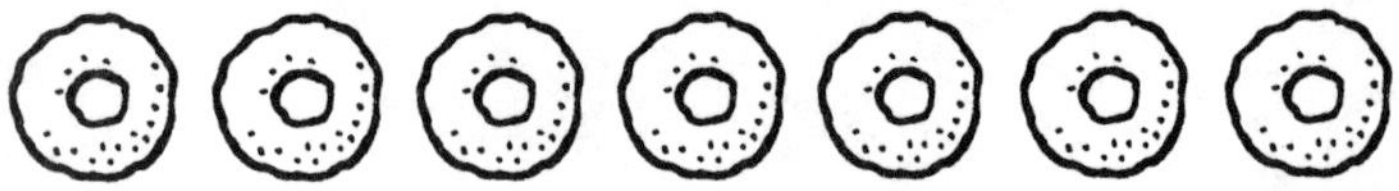

7 minus 4 is ______

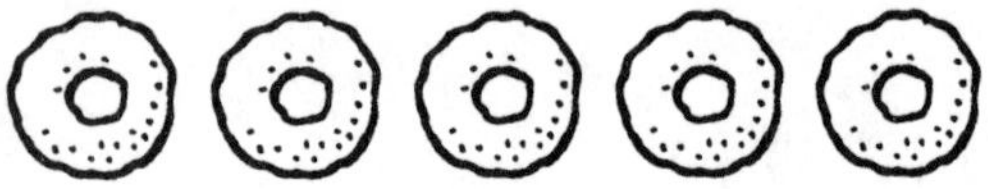

5 minus 1 is ______

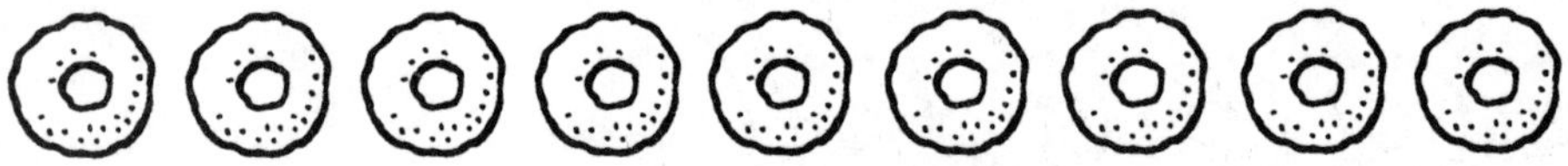

9 minus 5 is ______

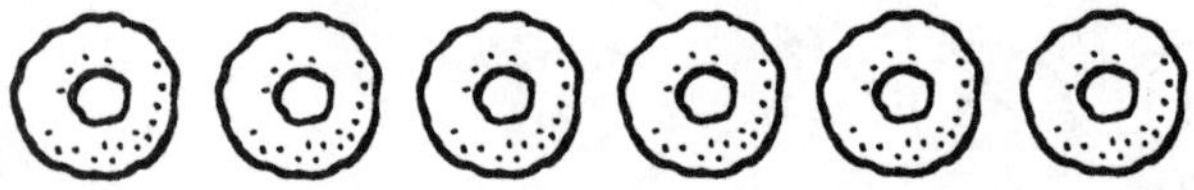

6 minus 3 is ______

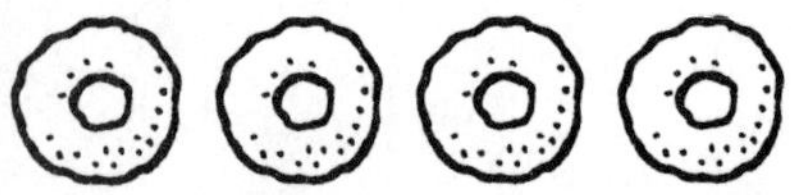

4 minus 3 is ______

Name _____

Solve the problems.

9   minus   6   is _____

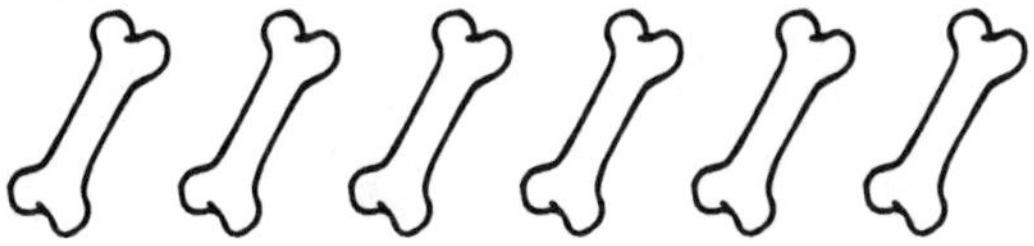

6   minus   4   is _____

4   minus   1   is _____

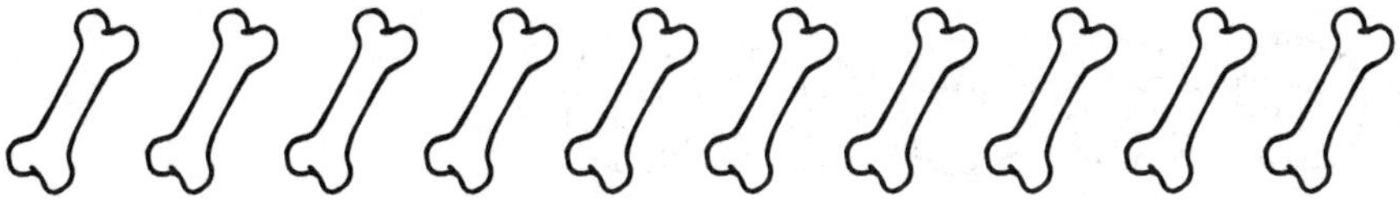

10   minus   5   is _____

7   minus   5   is _____

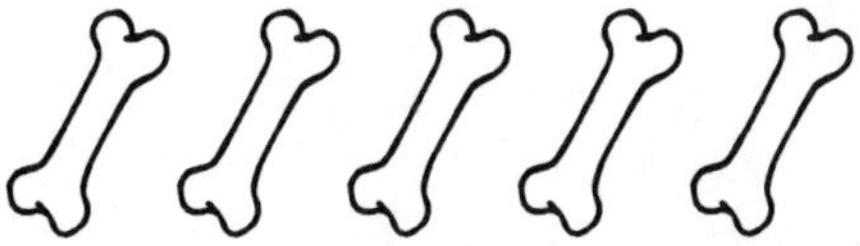

5   minus   2   is _____

Name _____

Solve the problems.

7   take away   1   is _____

5   take away   3   is _____

10   take away   9   is _____

6   take away   5   is _____

2   take away   1   is _____

9   take away   7   is _____

Name _____

Solve the problems.

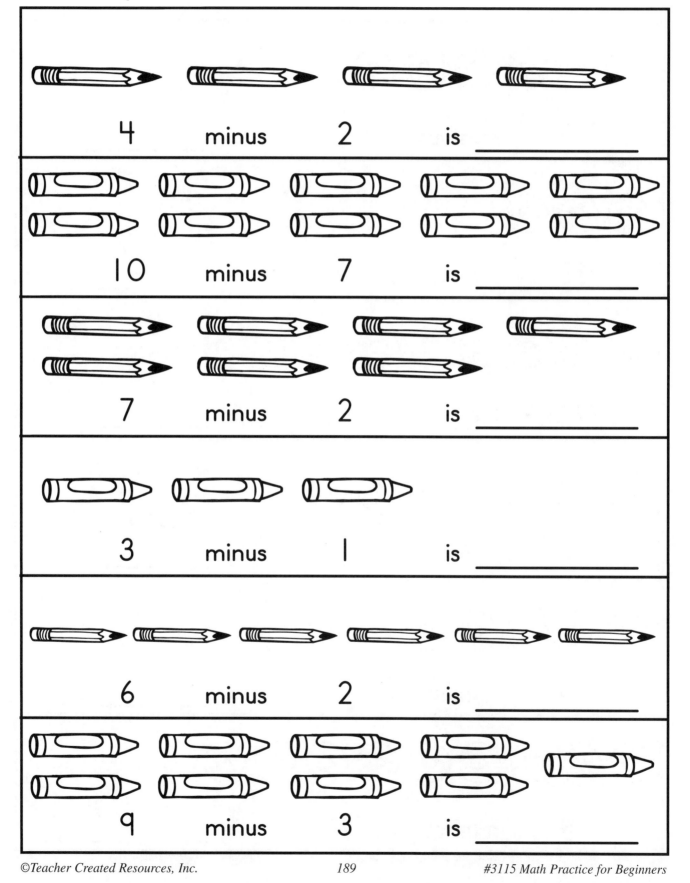

4 minus 2 is _____

10 minus 7 is _____

7 minus 2 is _____

3 minus 1 is _____

6 minus 2 is _____

9 minus 3 is _____

Name _____

Solve the problems.

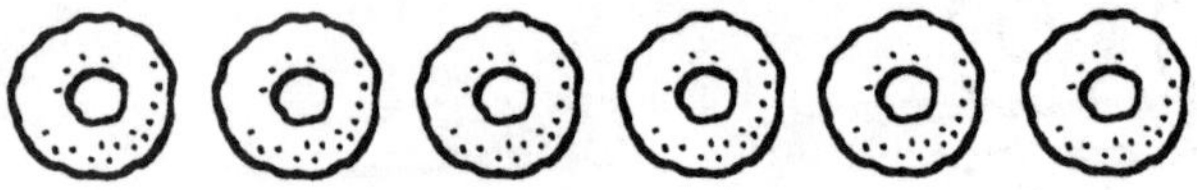

6   minus   2   is _____

3   minus   2   is _____

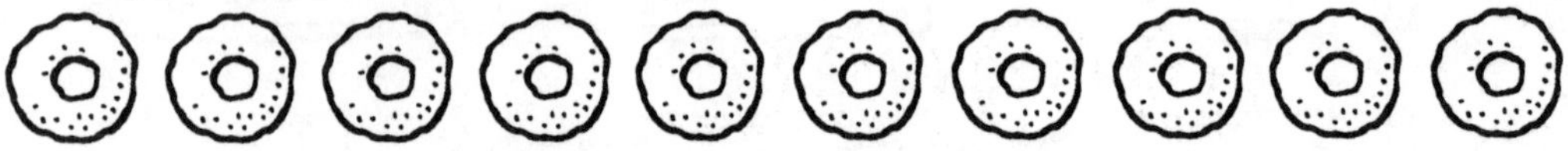

10   minus   8   is _____

7   minus   3   is _____

5   minus   4   is _____

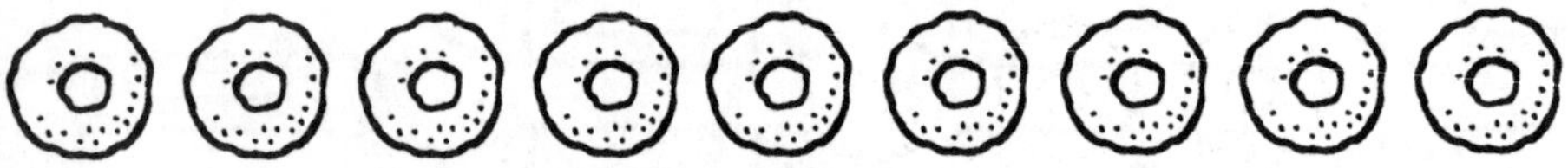

9   minus   8   is _____

Name _____

Count the circles. Write the sum on the line.

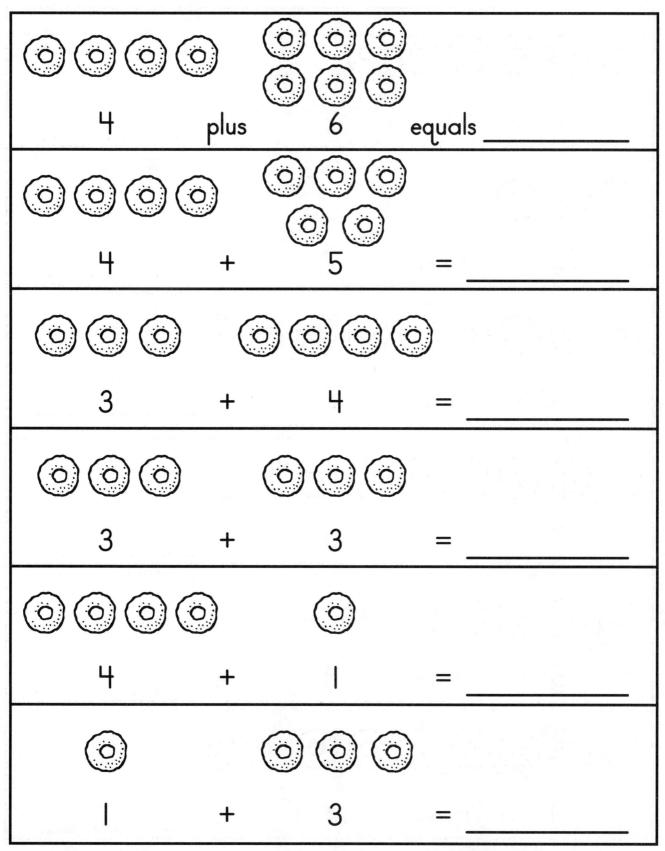

4   plus   6   equals _____

4   +   5   = _____

3   +   4   = _____

3   +   3   = _____

4   +   1   = _____

1   +   3   = _____

Name _____

Count the butterflies and flowers. Write the sum on the line.

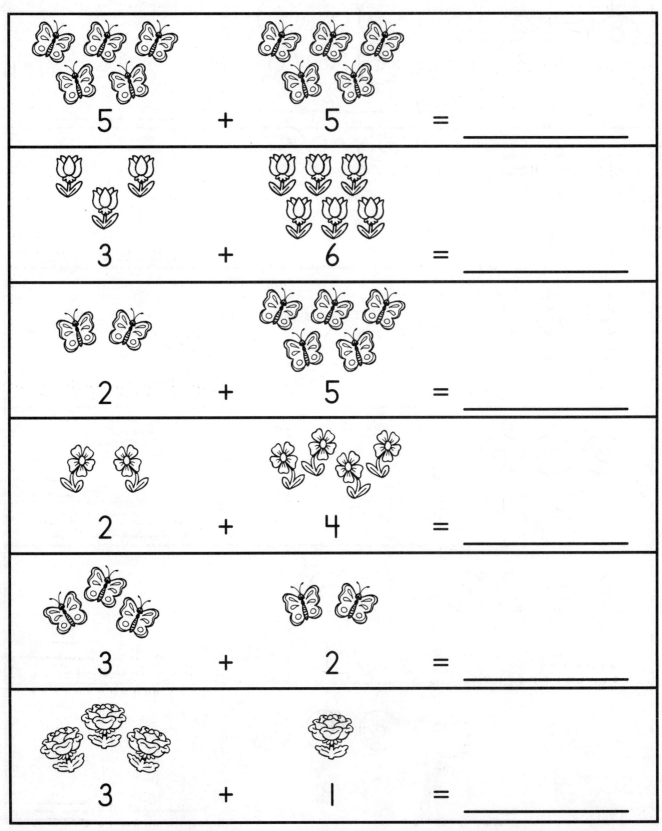

5 + 5 = _____

3 + 6 = _____

2 + 5 = _____

2 + 4 = _____

3 + 2 = _____

3 + 1 = _____

Name _____

Count the circles. Write the sum on the line.

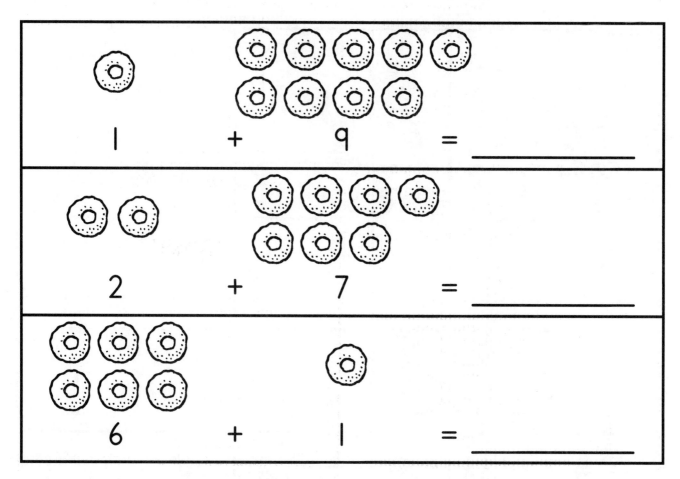

1   +   9   = _____

2   +   7   = _____

6   +   1   = _____

Write the sum below the line.

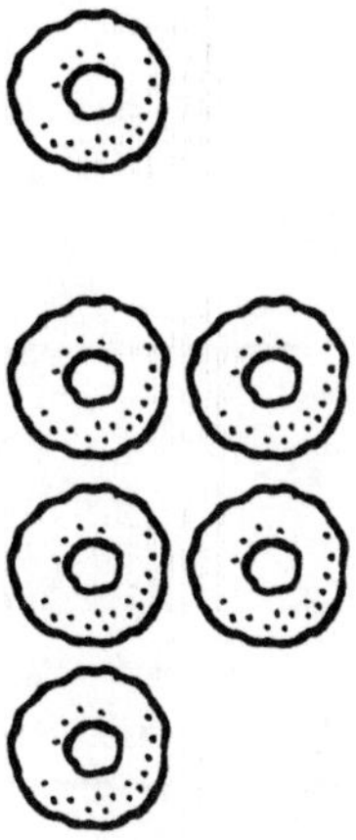

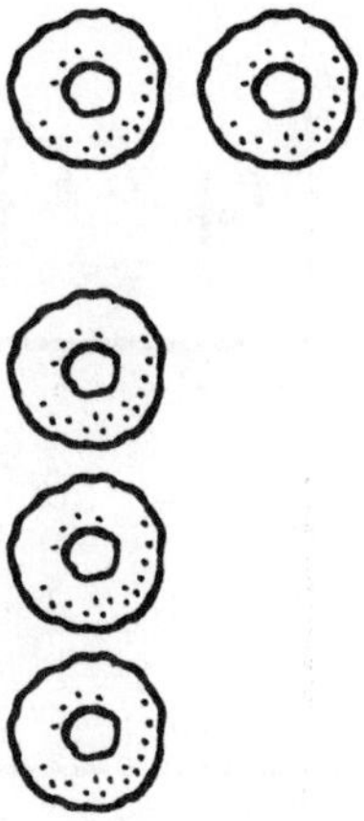

1
+ 5
____

2
+ 3
____

1
+ 1
____

Name _____

Count the hearts. Write the sum below the line.

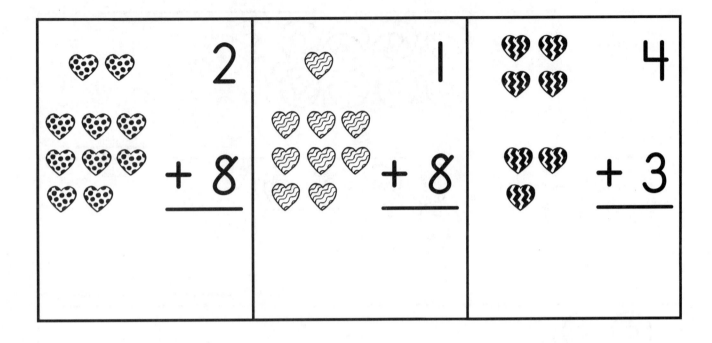

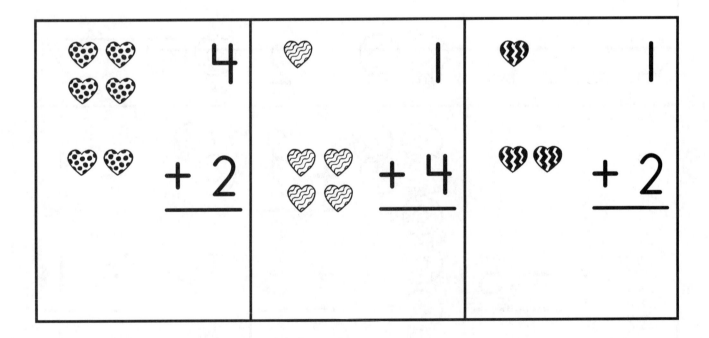

Name _____

Count the circles. Write the sum below the line.

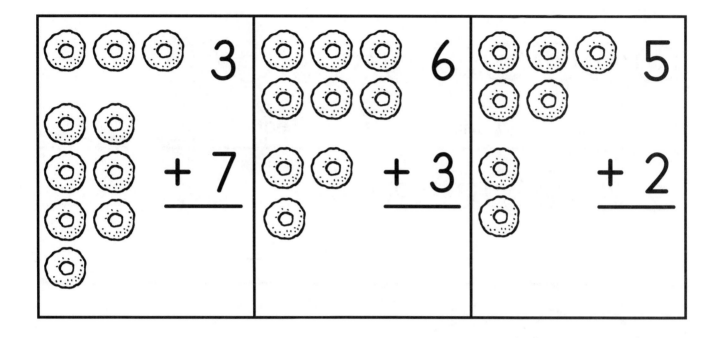

Name _____

Count the circles. Cross out the number to be subtracted. Write the remainder on the line.

○ ○ ○ ○ ○ ○ ○ ○ ○ ○

10   minus   6   equals _____

○ ○ ○ ○ ○ ○ ○

7   –   4   = _____

○ ○ ○ ○ ○

5   –   1   = _____

○ ○ ○ ○ ○ ○ ○ ○ ○

9   –   5   = _____

○ ○ ○ ○ ○ ○

6   –   3   = _____

○ ○ ○ ○

4   –   3   = _____

Name _____

Count the penguins and whales.
Cross out the number to be subtracted.
Write the remainder on the line.

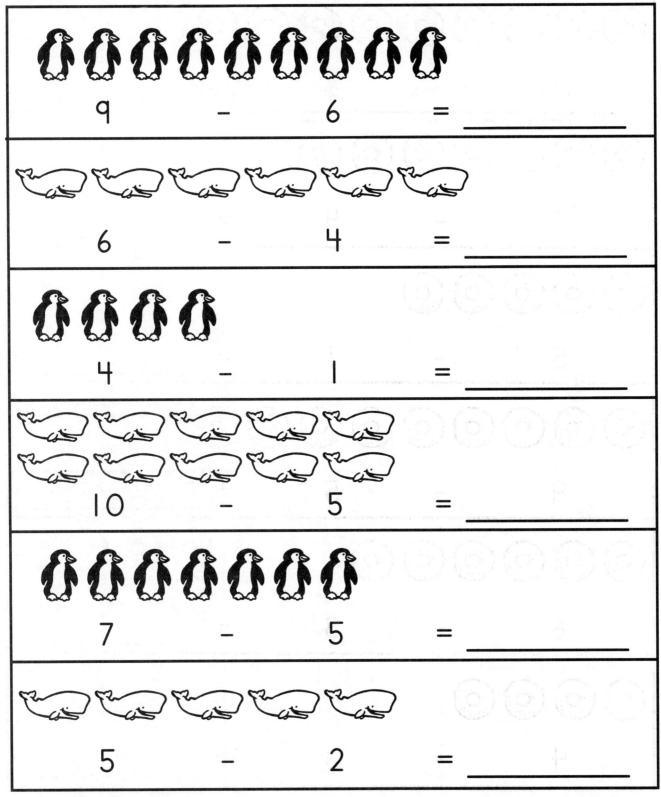

9   –   6   = _____

6   –   4   = _____

4   –   1   = _____

10   –   5   = _____

7   –   5   = _____

5   –   2   = _____

Name _____

Count the circles. Cross out the circles to be subtracted. Write the remainder on the line.

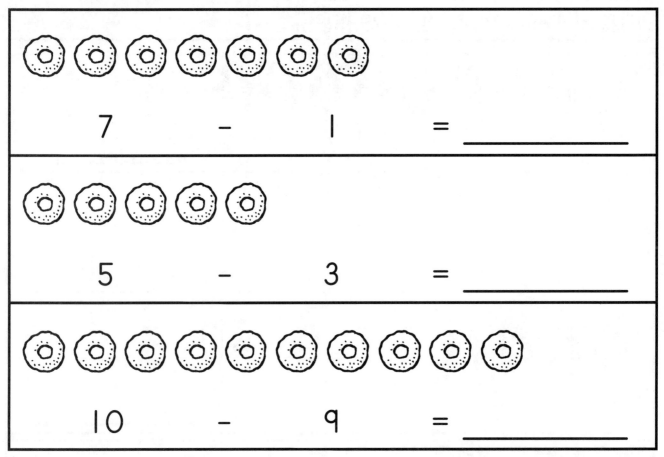

7   −   1   = _____

5   −   3   = _____

10   −   9   = _____

Write the remainder below the line.

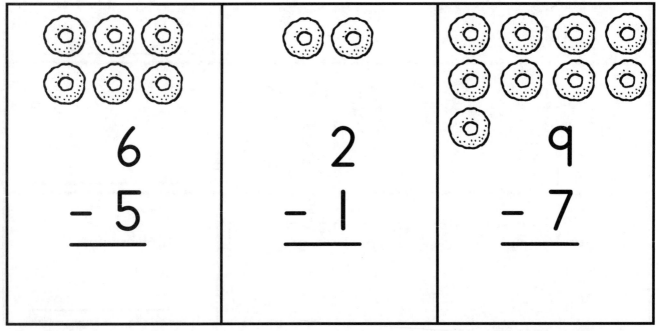

$$\begin{array}{r} 6 \\ -\ 5 \\ \hline \end{array}$$

$$\begin{array}{r} 2 \\ -\ 1 \\ \hline \end{array}$$

$$\begin{array}{r} 9 \\ -\ 7 \\ \hline \end{array}$$

Name _____

Count the kites.

Cross out the number to be subtracted.

Write the remainder below the line.

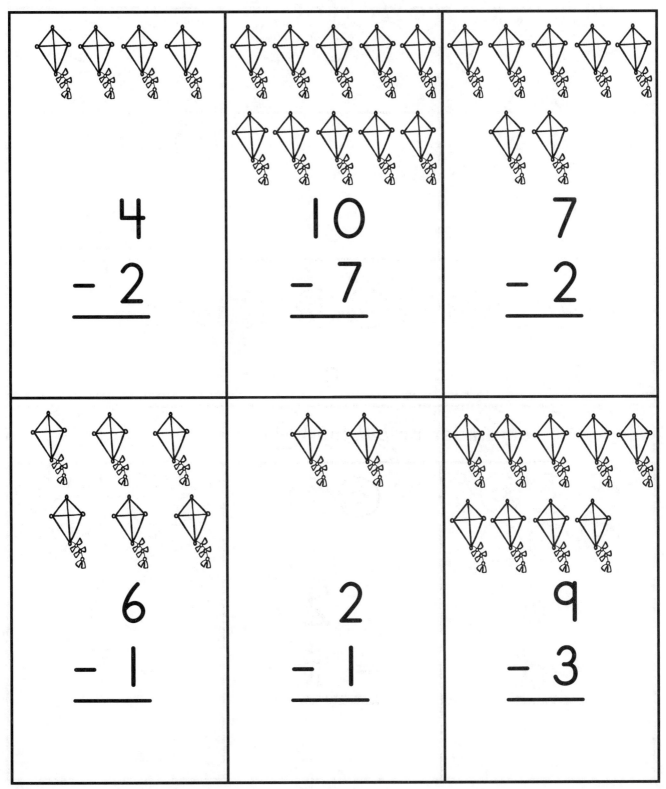

$$4 - 2$$

$$10 - 7$$

$$7 - 2$$

$$6 - 1$$

$$2 - 1$$

$$9 - 3$$

Name _____

Count the circles.

Cross out the number to be subtracted.

Write the remainder below the line.

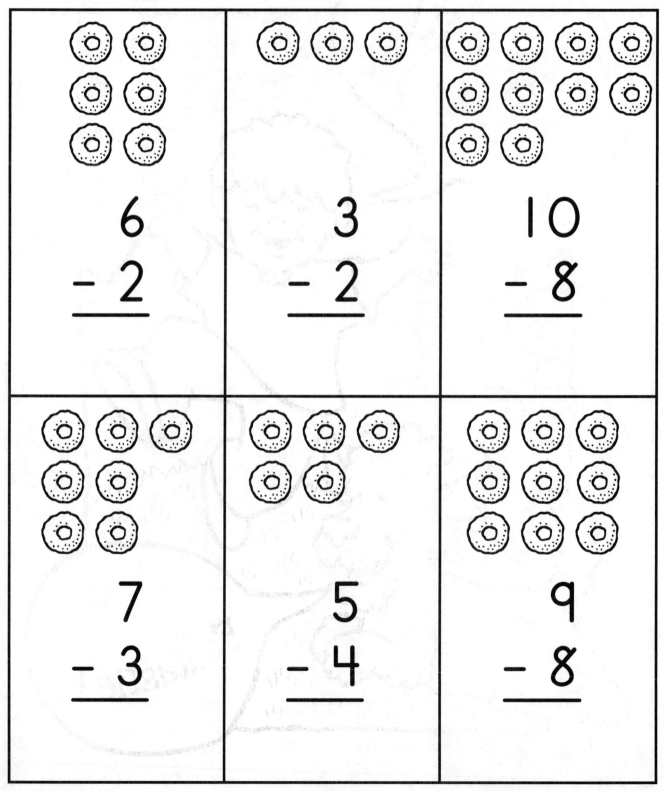

Name _____

Name _____

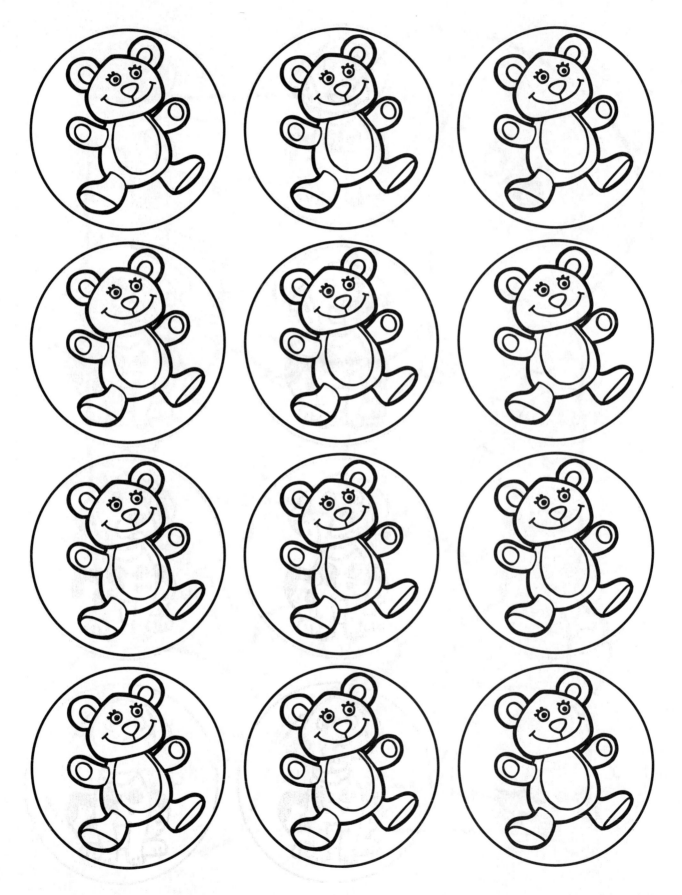

Name _____

Name _____

Name _____

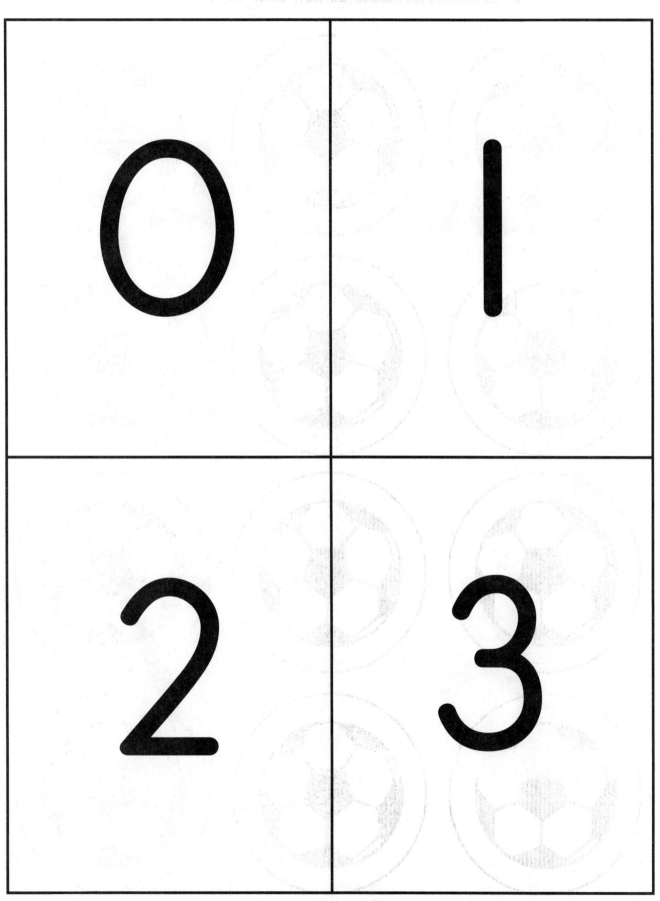

Name _____

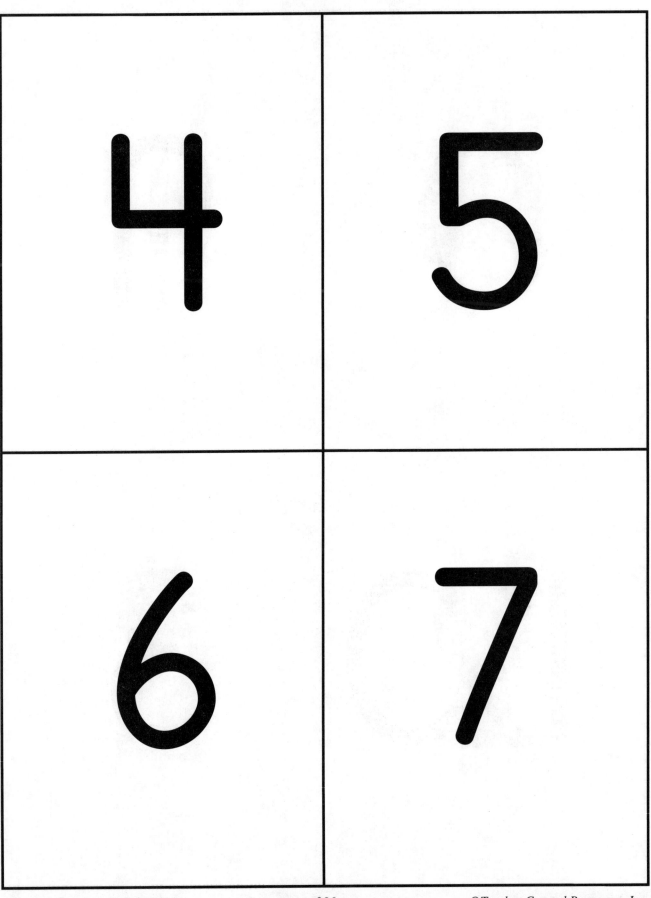

Name _____

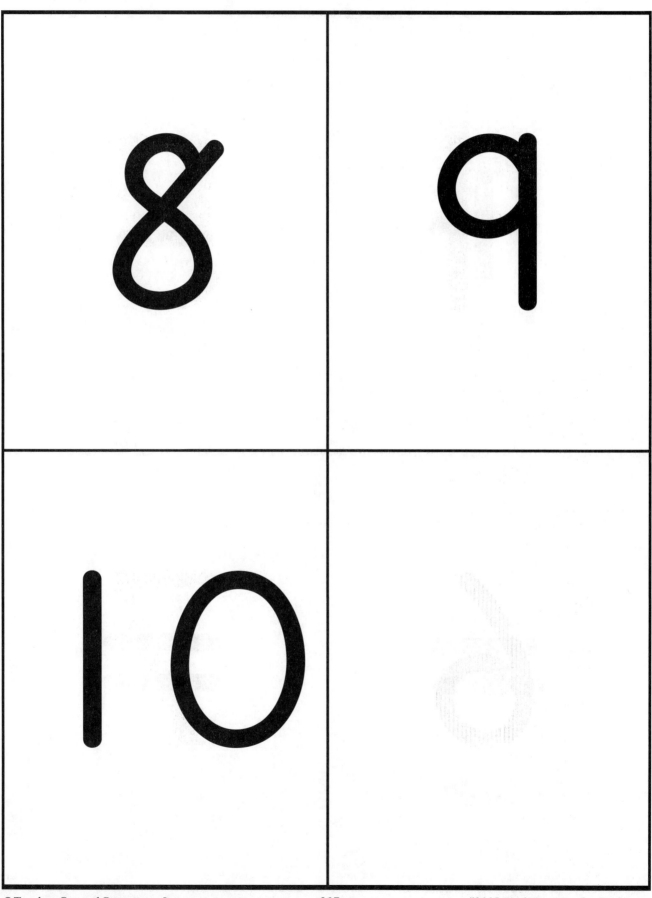

Name _____

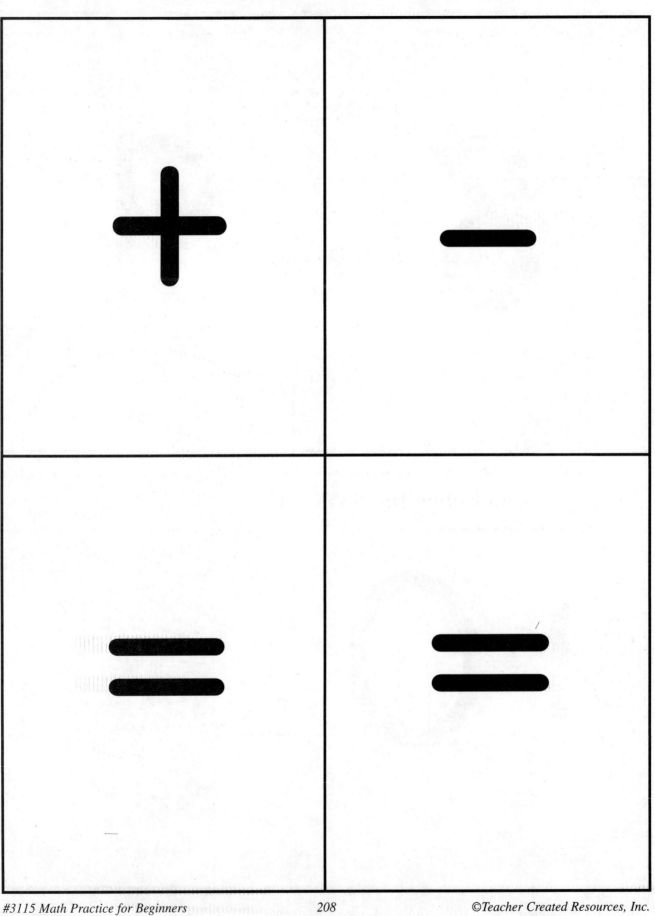